# HUMAN RIGHTS IN AFRICA

# HUMAN RIGHTS IN AFRICA

Brian Baughan

Mason Crest Publishers

Philadelphia

Frontispiece: The body of a woman killed by Hutu extremists lies on a street in Kayove, Rwanda, as soldiers of the rebel Rwandan Patriotic Front march through the town, June 16, 1994.

Produced by OTTN Publishing, Stockton, New Jersey

**Mason Crest Publishers**
370 Reed Road
Broomall, PA 19008
www.masoncrest.com

3 5 7 9 8 6 4 2

Library of Congress Cataloging-in-Publication Data

Baughan, Brian.
 Human rights / Brian Baughan.
   p. cm. — (Africa, progress and problems)
 Includes bibliographical references and index.
 ISBN-13: 978-1-59084-960-6
 ISBN-10: 1-59084-960-4
 1. Human rights—Africa. I. Title. II. Series.
 JC599.A36B38 2006
 323.4'9'096—dc22
                                    2005016305

# TABLE OF CONTENTS

# ≋ AFRICA: PROGRESS & PROBLEMS ≋

AIDS AND HEALTH ISSUES

CIVIL WARS IN AFRICA

ECOLOGICAL ISSUES

EDUCATION IN AFRICA

ETHNIC GROUPS IN AFRICA

GOVERNANCE AND LEADERSHIP
IN AFRICA

HELPING AFRICA HELP ITSELF:
A GLOBAL EFFORT

HUMAN RIGHTS IN AFRICA

ISLAM IN AFRICA

THE MAKING OF MODERN AFRICA

POPULATION AND OVERCROWDING

POVERTY AND ECONOMIC ISSUES

RELIGIONS OF AFRICA

# THE PROMISE OF TODAY'S AFRICA

## by Robert I. Rotberg

Today's Africa is a mosaic of effective democracy and desperate despotism, immense wealth and abysmal poverty, conscious modernity and mired traditionalism, bitter conflict and vast arenas of peace, and enormous promise and abiding failure. Generalizations are more difficult to apply to Africa or Africans than elsewhere. The continent, especially the sub-Saharan two-thirds of its immense landmass, presents enormous physical, political, and human variety. From snow-capped peaks to intricate patches of remaining jungle, from desolate deserts to the greatest rivers, and from the highest coastal sand dunes anywhere to teeming urban conglomerations, Africa must be appreciated from myriad perspectives. Likewise, its peoples come in every shape and size, govern themselves in several complicated manners, worship a host of indigenous and imported gods, and speak thousands of original and five or six derivative common languages. To know Africa is to know nuance and complexity.

There are 53 nation-states that belong to the African Union, 48 of which are situated within the sub-Saharan mainland or on its offshore islands. No other continent has so many countries, political divisions, or members of the General Assembly of the United Nations. No other continent encompasses so many distinctively different peoples or spans such geographical disparity. On no other continent have so many innocent civilians lost their lives in intractable civil wars—12 million since 1991 in such places as Algeria, Angola, the Congo, Côte d'Ivoire, Liberia, Sierra Leone, and the Sudan. No other continent has so many disparate natural resources (from cadmium, cobalt, and copper to petroleum and zinc) and so little to show for their frenzied exploitation. No other continent has proportionally so many people subsisting (or trying to) on less than $1 a day. But then no other continent has been so beset by HIV/AIDS (30 percent of all adults in southern Africa), by tuberculosis, by malaria (prevalent almost everywhere), and by less well-known scourges such as schistosomiasis (liver fluke), several kinds of filariasis, river blindness, trachoma, and trypanosomiasis (sleeping sickness).

Africa is the most Christian continent. It has more Muslims than the Middle East. Apostolic and Pentecostal churches are immensely powerful. So are Sufi brotherhoods. Yet traditional African religions are still influential. So is a belief in spirits and witches (even among Christians and Muslims), in faith healing and in alternative medicine. Polygamy remains popular. So does the practice of female circumcision and other long-standing cultural preferences. Africa cannot be well understood without appreciating how village life still permeates the great cities and how urban pursuits engulf villages. Half if not more of its peoples live in towns and cities; no longer can Africa be considered predominantly rural, agricultural, or wild.

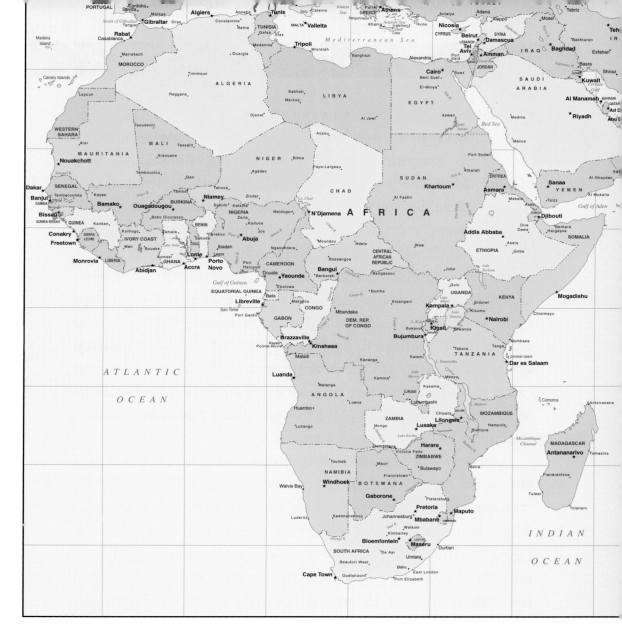

Political leaders must cater to both worlds, old and new. They and their followers must join the globalized, Internet-penetrated world even as they remain rooted appropriately in past modes of behavior, obedient to dictates of family, lineage, tribe, and ethnicity. This duality often results in democracy or at

least partially participatory democracy. Equally often it develops into autocracy. Botswana and Mauritius have enduring democratic governments. In Benin, Ghana, Kenya, Lesotho, Malawi, Mali, Mozambique, Namibia, Nigeria, Senegal, South Africa, Tanzania, and Zambia fully democratic pursuits are relatively recent and not yet sustainably implanted. Algeria, Cameroon, Chad, the Central African Republic, Egypt, the Sudan, and Tunisia are authoritarian entities run by strongmen. Zimbabweans and Equatorial Guineans suffer from even more venal rule. Swazis and Moroccans are subject to the real whims of monarchs. Within even this vast sweep of political practice there are still more distinctions. The partial democracies represent a spectrum. So does the manner in which authority is wielded by kings, by generals, and by long-entrenched civilian autocrats.

The democratic countries are by and large better developed and more rapidly growing economically than those ruled by strongmen. In Africa there is an association between the pursuit of good governance and beneficial economic performance. Likewise, the natural resource wealth curse that has afflicted mineral-rich countries such as the Congo and Nigeria has had the opposite effect in well-governed places like Botswana. Nation-states open to global trade have done better than those with closed economies. So have those countries with prudent managements, sensible fiscal arrangements, and modest deficits. Overall, however, the bulk of African countries have suffered in terms of reduced economic growth from the sheer fact of being tropical, beset by disease in an enervating climate

where there is an average of one trained physician to every 13,000 persons. Many lose growth prospects, too, because of the absence of navigable rivers, the paucity of ocean and river ports, barely maintained roads, and few and narrow railroads. Moreover, 15 of Africa's countries are landlocked, without comfortable access to relatively inexpensive waterborne transport. Hence, imports and exports for much of Africa are more expensive than elsewhere as they move over formidable distances. Africa is the most underdeveloped continent because of geographical and health constraints that have not yet been overcome, because of ill-considered policies, because of the sheer number of separate nation-states (a colonial legacy), and because of poor governance.

Africa's promise is immense, and far more exciting than its achievements have been since a wave of nationalism and independence in the 1960s liberated nearly every section of the continent. Thus, the next several decades of the 21st century are ones of promise for Africa. The challenges are clear: to alleviate grinding poverty and deliver greater real economic goods to larger proportions of people in each country, and across all 53 countries; to deliver more of the benefits of good governance to more of Africa's peoples; to end the destructive killing fields that run rampant across so much of Africa; to improve educational training and health services; and to roll back the scourges of HIV/AIDS, tuberculosis, and malaria. Every challenge represents an opportunity with concerted and bountiful Western assistance to transform the lives of Africa's vulnerable and resourceful future generations.

# HOLLOW PROMISES?

Moments after they killed her husband, two Sudanese militiamen forced Zahara Abdulkarim to the ground and raped her. "They also wanted to kill me," she remembered, "but when they saw I was pregnant, they released me and let me live." Before completing their raid on Ablieh, a small town located in the Darfur region of western Sudan, they also killed four of Abdulkarim's in-laws and two of her sons. This attack was one in a long series that Arab militias known as the Janjaweed had waged on Darfur's black civilians, beginning in February 2003 and continuing into 2006.

By August 2004, the month that Zahara Abdulkarim's story was included in a *Time* magazine article, an estimated 50,000 people of Darfur had been killed and 1.4 million had been displaced. By April 2005 the Coalition for International Justice estimated that the number of people killed in Darfur had reached 140,000, and that an additional 260,000 had succumbed to disease, malnutrition, dehydration, heatstroke, or other causes attributable to dislocations caused by the violence. Clearly, human rights were being violated in Darfur on a massive scale.

# FUNDAMENTAL CLAIMS

Human rights are the fundamental claims to which every individual is entitled. If a government cannot (or will not) secure these claims for its people, justice and freedom are also unattainable. A right is either stated as an expression of an individual entitlement or as a protection from an external force. In other words, a right may be the ability to exercise a certain freedom (such as freedom to practice a religion, express one's political views, or associate with a group of people), or it may be a protection from improper or unlawful treatment at the hands of an individual, group, or government (such as discrimination, arbitrary arrest, or torture).

The idea that all human beings are entitled to certain rights has existed for centuries—though views on precisely which rights should be considered fundamental have varied, and in any case governments have not always protected and promoted these rights. Fundamental rights have gone by different names, but they have been widely known as human rights only since 1948, the year the United Nations adopted and proclaimed the Universal Declaration of Human Rights. This declaration, which has been signed by all 191 of the UN member states, is the international standard on fundamental freedoms. Other declarations, ratified by regional and national organizations, pledge that the rights declared at the global level will be protected in a particular region or country.

While securing human rights is a universal concern, people around the world have often wrestled over the question of how certain rights categories (for example, political, economic, cultural, collective) relate to one another, and whether one category should take precedence over the others. Nonetheless, some rights are recognized as the most basic and indispensable. Among these are the right to life, liberty, and security of person—rights enshrined in Article 3 of the Universal Declaration of Human Rights.

In Africa and the rest of the world, leaders are well aware of their obligations to promote and protect these rights. The global human rights system contains national, regional, and international components. National leaders are committed to acknowledge and safeguard the human rights of their people through the various conventions, charters, and treaties of which their

## ASSESSING BASIC FREEDOMS

Human rights, unlike issues such as poverty or AIDS, is an abstract concept for which numerical indicators are rarely cited. However, one research group, Freedom House, has attempted to paint an objective picture of the status of rights around the world through its ratings system. Every year it assesses "the progress and decline of political rights and civil liberties" in 192 countries and assigns them ratings between 1 (denoting most free) and 7 (least free).

While useful, the Freedom House ratings should not be taken as definitive measures, as they focus on just two (albeit very important) categories of human rights. That said, the Freedom House evaluation of Africa is not favorable. Of the 52 African countries that were evaluated in 2005, a mere 11 were classified as "free," and only 23 were rated "partly free." Worldwide, 45 countries received Freedom House's "not free" rating, and 18 of them— 40 percent of the total—were African.

African states with exceptionally bad Freedom House ratings included Equatorial Guinea (7 for political rights; 6 for civil liberties) in West Africa; Zimbabwe (7/6) in southern Africa; Somalia (6/7) on the Horn of Africa; the Democratic Republic of the Congo (6/6) in central Africa; and Libya and Sudan (both 7/7) in northern Africa. As this sample group shows, at least one country in every major African region was found to suffer from large-scale rights abuse. By contrast, Cape Verde was the only African nation among the 50 countries receiving Freedom House's highest rating (1 in political rights and 1 in civil liberties).

countries are signatories. In addition, many countries, including about 25 in Africa, have established national human rights commissions. At the regional level, organizations such as the African Union, the Council of Europe, and the Organization of American States (which embraces the entire Western Hemisphere) have bodies dedicated to human rights protection. Internationally, the United Nations advances the cause of human rights through the Office of the High Commissioner for Human Rights (OHCHR), which is assisted by various UN organs, including the Security Council, the High Commissioner for Refugees, and the Development Program.

## SYSTEMIC FAILURES

In theory, then, a legal and administrative framework was in place to protect the human rights of residents of Sudan's Darfur region—or at least to respond effectively when large-scale violations of those rights began occurring in 2003. Few observers would argue that Darfurians enjoyed any meaningful protection, however. For three years Sudanese Arab militiamen were virtually unimpeded as they kept up their brutal campaign against Darfur's black population. The armed and horse-mounted Janjaweed descended on hapless villages, setting buildings and food sources on fire, slaughtering livestock, murdering, raping, looting, and even abducting villagers for slaves.

As early as March 2003, a United Nations official correctly identified one of the primary goals of the Janjaweed's terror campaign—"ethnic cleansing," or the expulsion of a minority group from their land through violent tactics such as intimidation, rape, and murder. "This is ethnic cleansing, . . . and I don't know why the world is not doing more about it," railed Mukesh Kapila, the UN humanitarian coordinator for Sudan.

As reports of the atrocities in Darfur poured in, human rights groups and various U.S. leaders—including members of

Congress, President George W. Bush, and Secretary of State Colin Powell—called the attacks acts of genocide. That is not a term world leaders use lightly, as a UN convention to which more than 135 countries, including the United States, are party requires states to "undertake to prevent and to punish" the crime of genocide.

The United Nations Security Council issued four separate resolutions urging the government to end the attacks on civilians; the UN also sent an international commission to Sudan in November 2004 to observe firsthand what was taking place. The commission ended its inquiry three months later, concluding that what had happened was not genocide, though serious crimes under international law had been committed.

In late 2004 the first soldiers from an African Union peacekeeping force began arriving in Darfur. But the AU contingent never exceeded about 7,800 troops, a number insufficient to patrol an area the size of Texas—particularly since the soldiers were lightly armed, lacked logistical support, and were burdened with rules of engagement that did not permit them to disarm militias or even to fight to protect civilians under attack.

In March 2005 the United Nations Security Council—the high-level UN body vested with primary responsibility for maintaining international peace and security—referred the Darfur situation to the International Criminal Court (ICC). Created by the Rome Statute and headquartered in The Hague, the ICC—which came into existence in 2002—is a permanent court that has jurisdiction to prosecute genocide, crimes against humanity, and war crimes when the justice systems of individual states cannot or will not prosecute those offenses. As the chief prosecutor of the ICC launched an investigation into crimes in Darfur—an investigation that he conceded would "require sustained cooperation from national and international authorities"—the large-scale murder, rape, and pillaging in Sudan continued.

In September 2005 the UN's member states unanimously agreed to accept responsibility for protecting populations from ethnic cleansing, genocide, war crimes, and crimes against humanity. But the statement of the General Assembly, the UN's main deliberative body, was nonbinding and had little impact in Darfur. By early 2006, when the Janjaweed militias began crossing into neighboring Chad to attack refugee camps and Chadian civilians, the number of Darfurians killed had reached an estimated 200,000, and at least 2 million others had been forced from their homes. Meanwhile, the Sudanese government was accused of making a concerted effort to prevent humanitarian aid from reaching displaced Darfurians.

In March 2006, under pressure from the United States and the European Union, the African Union agreed in principle to hand over the Darfur peacekeeping mission to the UN, which would presumably field a larger and better-equipped force. But under even the most optimistic scenarios, it would take a minimum of six months before any UN force was in place. And Sudan's president, Omar al-Bashir, said his country would never accept UN peacekeepers in Darfur.

With Darfur's agony entering its fourth year, Darfurians and human rights advocates all over the globe expressed exasperation at the international community's response to the situation. Despite frequent pronouncements that serious crimes against international law had occurred or were occurring in the western part of Sudan, and despite acknowledging its collective responsibility to prevent those very crimes, the international community had failed to take the kind of forceful, concerted action that might stop the atrocities in Darfur. How could this happen? Why were the atrocities in Sudan allowed to continue for so long?

The answers to these questions reveal major shortcomings in the international human rights system and cast light on why Africa has been particularly vulnerable to rights abuses. The

The Darfur crisis was the focus of this May 2006 United Nations Security Council session. While the UN repeatedly condemned the human rights abuses committed in Darfur—and some world leaders, including U.S. president George W. Bush, even characterized those abuses as genocide—the international community failed to muster the will to stop the atrocities.

unfortunate reality is that rights guarantees like those found in the Universal Declaration of Human Rights mean little in the absence of meaningful enforcement mechanisms. The United Nations—while it might pass resolutions that censure, or impose sanctions on, a government for human rights violations—has been loath to intervene militarily in the affairs of sovereign states, even in the midst of an ongoing humanitarian crisis. Regional organizations such as the African Union typically also share that reluctance, as do individual states (unless they perceive their vital national interests to be at stake). Thus the status of human rights in a particular country often boils down to how committed the government is to securing those rights for its citizens.

*(continued on p. 22)*

# EXCERPTS FROM THE UNIVERSAL DECLARATION OF HUMAN RIGHTS

**Article 1.**

All human beings are born free and equal in dignity and rights. . . .

**Article 3.**

Everyone has the right to life, liberty and security of person.

**Article 4.**

No one shall be held in slavery or servitude; slavery and the slave trade shall be prohibited in all their forms.

**Article 5.**

No one shall be subjected to torture or to cruel, inhuman or degrading treatment or punishment.

**Article 7.**

All are equal before the law and are entitled without any discrimination to equal protection of the law. . . .

**Article 9.**

No one shall be subjected to arbitrary arrest, detention or exile.

**Article 11.**

(1) Everyone charged with a penal offence has the right to be presumed innocent until proved guilty according to law in a public trial at which he has had all the guarantees necessary for his defence.

**Article 13.**

(1) Everyone has the right to freedom of movement and residence within the borders of each state.

(2) Everyone has the right to leave any country, including his own, and to return to his country.

**Article 14.**

(1) Everyone has the right to seek and to enjoy in other countries asylum from persecution.

**Article 16.**

(1) Men and women of full age, without any limitation due to race, nationality or religion, have the right to marry and to found a family. They are entitled to equal rights as to marriage, during marriage and at its dissolution.

**Article 18.**

Everyone has the right to freedom of thought, conscience and religion. . . .

**Article 19.**

Everyone has the right to freedom of opinion and expression . . . and to seek, receive and impart information and ideas through any media and regardless of frontiers.

**Article 20.**

(1) Everyone has the right to freedom of peaceful assembly and association.

(2) No one may be compelled to belong to an association.

**Article 21.**

(1) Everyone has the right to take part in the government of his country, directly or through freely chosen representatives.

(3) The will of the people shall be the basis of the authority of government; this will shall be expressed in periodic and genuine elections which shall be by universal and equal suffrage. . . .

**Article 23.**

(1) Everyone has the right to work, to free choice of employment, to just and favourable conditions of work and to protection against unemployment.

(2) Everyone, without any discrimination, has the right to equal pay for equal work.

(3) Everyone who works has the right to just and favourable remuneration. . . .

(4) Everyone has the right to form and to join trade unions for the protection of his interests.

**Article 26.**

(1) Everyone has the right to education. . . .

In the case of Sudan, the regime of President Omar al-Bashir was complicit in—and probably helped direct—the atrocities perpetrated by the Janjaweed militias. Government planes and helicopters regularly bombed and strafed Darfur's towns and villages. The government claimed that its targets were insurgents of the Sudanese Liberation Army (SLA), which was fighting to win autonomy for Darfur. Often, however, the aerial attacks immediately preceded Janjaweed raids, lending credence to charges that the government was coordinating the militias' campaign of terror against defenseless civilians.

Sudan's Arab- and Muslim-dominated government, whose base of power lies in the northern part of the country, had employed similar tactics before, in its long-running war against mostly non-Arab Christian and animist rebel forces from the south. An estimated 2 million people died as a result of the fighting, which began in 1983 as a continuation of a war that started in 1956; an additional 4 million were displaced by the conflict. In January 2005, the government and southern rebels finally signed a peace agreement, although Darfur was excluded from those negotiations.

If Sudan has witnessed rampant and recurring abuses of the most basic human rights, it is by no means unique among African countries. A

A camp for internally displaced persons in Geneina, Sudan. The violence in Darfur has forced more than 2 million people from their homes.

Pro-government demonstrators in Khartoum protest a July 2004 UN Security Council resolution calling on the Sudanese government to disarm the Janjaweed militias. The Sudanese government ignored that resolution, just as it thwarted other international attempts to end the violence in Darfur. The crisis in western Sudan exposed, once again, a critical weakness in the international system for protecting human rights. The only course of action guaranteed to stop rights violations committed by the government of a sovereign nation within its own borders is military intervention, and the international community is extremely reluctant to resort to that option.

decade before the Darfur killings began, about 800,000 members of Rwanda's Tutsi minority were massacred in three short months as the world basically stood by. During the period between these two calamities, innocent civilians from every major region of Africa became the victims of the worst kinds of abuse. That so many human rights violations, both blatant and little noticed, occur in Africa speaks volumes about the international community's lack of resolve in enforcing its highest principles—and about the continuing failures of many of Africa's governments.

# AN EVOLVING PROCESS

**B**y definition, human rights belong to all people, regardless of gender, race, nationality, religion, or other individual circumstances. Human rights are not to be confused with privileges of citizenship; they are the entitlement of everyone and cannot legitimately be denied by any government.

The universality of certain rights was an important principle of the 18th-century Enlightenment, which formed the philosophical foundations of the first democratic revolutions, in America and France. These revolutions, in turn, influenced later struggles for freedom in many other nations.

While the language of universal, unalienable rights inspired the American and French Revolutions and their offspring, in certain respects reality failed to match rhetoric. The constitutions and bills of rights promulgated during the 18th and 19th centuries to guarantee fundamental rights and freedoms did not protect all people equally. The continuation of slavery in the United States and in France's colonies until the mid-1800s may be the most prominent example. But it must also be noted that, with the exception of New Zealand, in no country were women granted the right to vote until the 20th century. Today, women enjoy equal voting rights with men in all but a handful of countries, and slavery is illegal virtually everywhere. The idea that governments might condone slavery or deny voting rights to women now seems not just morally unacceptable but nearly inconceivable—testament to how far the common understanding of fundamental rights has evolved over the last centuries.

Ideas regarding the responsibility for protecting human rights have also evolved, if perhaps not quite so obviously. Until the mid-20th century, individual governments were generally seen as accountable only for securing the rights of their own citizens. While human rights were acknowledged as universal and unalienable, the failure of one government to grant such rights to its citizens was typically not seen as a matter of concern for other governments. That began to change in the aftermath of World War II. The conflict, which raged from 1939 to 1945, brought horrors on an unprecedented scale, including the systematic extermination by Nazi Germany of 6 million Jews and other so-called undesirables.

# CREATION OF THE INTERNATIONAL HUMAN RIGHTS SYSTEM

In December 1945 the United Nations was established in order to maintain international peace and security and, in the words of Article 1 of the organization's charter, "to achieve international cooperation . . . in promoting and encouraging respect for human rights and for fundamental freedoms for all. . . ." The state of human rights in a particular country would henceforth be considered a matter of international concern. At the same time, however,

Article 2 of the UN's charter stated, "The Organization is based on the principle of the Sovereign equality of all its members." In the years since the founding of the UN, the principle of national sovereignty has often collided with the ideal of upholding international human rights norms. Regimes that commit serious violations of human rights won't necessarily respond to moral persuasion or even diplomatic and economic sanctions. The final option available to the international community—military intervention—has been used only rarely to stop human rights abuses.

In 1948 the United Nations General Assembly adopted the Universal Declaration of Human Rights by unanimous vote, with the countries of the Soviet bloc and Saudi Arabia abstaining. (UN declarations are not legally binding, however.) The document's 30 articles enumerate the fundamental human rights and freedoms that, according to the preamble, collectively constitute "a common standard of achievement for all peoples and all nations." Many are the sorts of civil and political rights that had been familiar since the American Revolution and the framing of the U.S. Constitution in the late 18th century (including the right to life, liberty, and security of person; freedom of thought, conscience, and religion; freedom from arbitrary arrest; the right to a fair trial and the presumption of innocence when charged with a crime; and freedom from torture or cruel or degrading punishment).

But the Universal Declaration of Human Rights significantly broadened the traditional understanding of fundamental rights and freedoms. The declaration defined as human rights what previously might have been considered economic, social, and cultural ideals. For example, Article 23 stated, in part, "Everyone has the right to work, to free choice of employment, to just and favourable conditions of work and to protection against unemployment." Article 24 set forth a universal right "to rest and leisure, including reasonable limitation of working hours and periodic holidays with pay." Article 26 stated, in part, "Everyone has the right to education. Education shall be free, at least in the elementary and fundamental stages. Elementary education shall be compulsory. Technical and professional education shall be made generally available and higher education shall be equally accessible to all on the basis of merit." In the words of Article 27, "Everyone has the right freely to participate in the cultural life of the community, to enjoy the arts and to share in scientific advancement and its benefits."

## HUMAN RIGHTS IN AFRICA BEFORE INDEPENDENCE

At the time the United Nations drafted the Universal Declaration of Human Rights, most of Africa remained under the control of European powers, which had carved up the continent (largely during the late 19th century) into numerous colonies and protectorates. In the immediate aftermath of World War II there were only a handful of independent African states: Egypt, Ethiopia, Liberia. Thus Africans had little direct input during the initial stage in the establishment of the international human rights system. However, this did not give the European powers license to continue denying the human rights of Africans under their rule—as they had done to varying degrees throughout the colonial era. (In fact, in the Universal Declaration of Human Rights, all UN member states acknowledged their obligation to secure the recognition and observance of human rights, "both among the peoples of Member States themselves and among the peoples of territories under their jurisdiction.") Nor did it mean that African nations could not commit formally to the international human rights system after they gained independence from the European colonial powers. The intent of the United Nations was not to invent new standards of conduct but rather to institutionalize universal principles of human dignity.

After World War II, momentum built for the decolonization of Africa. Great Britain—which along with France was the primary colonial power on the continent—had publicly committed to the principle of self-determination for all peoples in August 1941, when British prime minister Winston Churchill and U.S. president Franklin D. Roosevelt signed the Atlantic Charter. In 1944 two influential African leaders, Kwame Nkrumah of the Gold Coast (now Ghana) and Jomo Kenyatta of Kenya, helped form the Pan-African Federation, which united various groups in demanding autonomy for all of Africa's peoples. By the late 1940s, anti-colonial political parties and nationalist movements burgeoned from one end of the continent to the other.

The road to independence proved long and difficult for many African nations. Nevertheless, by 1975 the entire continent had

**Giants of African independence: Jomo Kenyatta (left) and Kwame Nkrumah. The two were instrumental in the formation of the Pan-African Federation and led their respective countries, Kenya and Ghana, to independence.**

cast off colonial rule, with the exception of the sparsely populated territory of Western Sahara; tiny Djibouti, near the Horn of Africa; the Seychelles, an island nation in the Indian Ocean; and the so-called settler colonies of southern Africa (Namibia, Rhodesia, and South Africa), where the descendants of white European settlers ruled by denying political rights to black majorities. Sometimes the end of colonial rule came only after a bloody war—as, for example, in Algeria, Cameroon, Kenya, Mozambique, and Angola. But in most cases, comparatively little violence accompanied the transition to independence.

It would be incorrect to suggest that colonial rule had affected people throughout the vast continent of Africa identically. To begin with, the administrative approaches of the European colonial powers—France, Great Britain, Germany, Portugal, and Belgium—had varied considerably. For instance, Great Britain—which sought to integrate its African possessions into a far-flung empire—had brought the rule of law and trained modest numbers of local people for civil service positions. Belgium, by contrast, was concerned chiefly with extracting natural resources from its immense Congo territory; it made no attempt to include Africans in the colonial administration and ruled with iron-fisted brutality. Despite the differences in their governing styles and strategies, however, the European nations shared the same motivation in colonizing Africa: to advance the interests of the mother country. The welfare of African subjects was a secondary concern, if it was considered at all. At minimum, subject peoples were denied basic political rights and freedoms, such as the right of self-determination; often the human rights abuses were nothing short of appalling.

Many Africans viewed independence as the solution to a host of problems, including human rights abuses. After they had won the right to self-determination, they reasoned, democracy, respect for citizens' rights, and even economic development would inevitably follow. This assumption was articulated by Kwame Nkrumah, prime minister and longtime president of Ghana, which in 1957 became the first nation in sub-Saharan Africa to gain independence. "Seek ye first the political kingdom," Nkrumah said, "and all other things will be added unto it."

# INDEPENDENCE: NO PANACEA

Unfortunately, independence did not spell an end to Africa's problems. A few countries, such as Botswana and Mauritius, succeeded in establishing stable, democratic governments with unwavering respect for human rights. More countries saw modest improvements in the area of basic rights, but all too often

## THE DEBATE OVER WHAT CONSTITUTES HUMAN RIGHTS

The articles of the Universal Declaration of Human Rights stood as general principles rather than enforceable laws for nearly two decades after the document's adoption by the General Assembly of the United Nations. It was not until the 1976 ratification of two agreements—the International Covenant on Civil and Political Rights and the International Covenant on Economic, Social and Cultural Rights—that the declaration became legally binding.

This long delay was largely the result of the Cold War, when the U.S.-led West and the Soviet-led Communist bloc struggled for geopolitical supremacy. The philosophical divide between the two camps extended to the question of which kinds of rights deserved the highest priority. Finally the UN's Western and Communist member states settled on a compromise, signing the two separate covenants. However, the West continued to focus on civil and political rights: freedom of thought, speech, and religion; the right to due process of the law and a fair trial; the right to peaceably assemble. These are known as first-generation rights because they were the first set of officially declared liberties, most famously contested for during the American and French revolutions of the late 18th century. Economic rights—which together with cultural and social rights are considered second-generation rights—took precedence for the Communist countries. Many of these rights were declared during the socialist revolutions of the 20th century.

In recent decades, many rights advocates aware of the developments in Africa these gains proved short-lived. In dozens of African countries the abuses of colonial rule were replicated—or even exceeded—by homegrown dictators and military regimes.

Several factors help explain the failure of democracy and human rights to take root in Africa in the years immediately following independence. The legacy of colonialism, some scholars contend, is largely to blame. Colonialism left many countries ill prepared for the challenges of independence. Their economies were underdeveloped and often overly reliant on the export of a few raw materials or agricultural commodities, leaving them highly vulnerable to fluctuations in world prices. The competition for economic resources has helped fuel considerable vio-

have reevaluated the old Western claim that second-generation rights are less important than political and civil rights. Economic rights, which for Nigerian scholar Osita Eze include "the right to work, to obtain social security, fair wages . . . to enjoy an adequate standard of living, [and] freedom from hunger," are all essential because they are "needed to sustain life." These rights claim high priority in many African countries, where development, poverty, and famine are often such critical issues.

The debate over political and economic rights subsided with the end of the Cold War in the early 1990s. As countries began to reexamine their overall approaches to human rights, there was increasing recognition of the interdependence of political rights and economic rights—and, in certain respects, international policies have found a closer balance between the two categories.

In recent years advocates—particularly in developing nations—have asserted that certain collective rights constitute another, long-neglected category of human rights. Dubbed "third-generation rights," these include the right to development, peace, a clean environment, and humanitarian assistance. The developing world's increased emphasis on third-generation rights is reflected, for example, in the Grand Bay Declaration, which was adopted in 1999 at the Organization of African Unity's First Ministerial Conference on Human Rights in Africa. The Grand Bay Declaration affirmed that "the right to development, the right to a generally satisfactory healthy environment and the right to national and international peace and security are universal and inalienable rights which form an integral part of fundamental human rights."

lence on the continent. In addition, in many places the colonial regimes had failed to educate a sufficient number of local people for the complexities of governing a modern state. Mozambique, for example, had only three dozen university graduates when it gained independence from Portugal in 1975. But that was more than the number of college graduates in the vast Belgian Congo at independence in 1960: two. Colonialism also left a legacy of serious ethnically based divisions and tensions, some scholars assert, because the colonial boundaries that became the basis for the borders of many independent African states brought together groups that had no history of cooperation with one another

Christian Herter, the U.S. secretary of state, greets Nigerian delegates to the United Nations, October 7, 1960. Nigeria had gained independence from Britain less than a week earlier. Many African leaders assumed that democracy and respect for human rights would inevitably follow the end of colonialism. But in Nigeria, as elsewhere on the continent, that belief proved overly optimistic.

and little perceived commonality of interest. In addition, some colonial administrations had favored one ethnic group over another as a technique of rule, which produced resentments among disfavored groups. In the post-independence period, many African leaders stoked intergroup tensions—and encouraged conflict and human rights abuses—by appealing to ethnic identity rather than national interest.

Another factor that contributed to Africa's dismal human rights record was the Cold War. During the period when African nations won independence from colonial rule, the United States and the Soviet Union were locked in a global struggle for supremacy. In Africa, as elsewhere in the developing world, the two superpowers funneled military and other aid to regimes and insurgent groups that were friendly to their interests. Client states and rebel groups supported by the United States or the Soviet Union frequently committed large-scale abuses, but for the Cold War adversaries, human rights in the Third World took a backseat to geopolitical advantage.

Perhaps the greatest stumbling blocks to human rights in postcolonial Africa, however, have been political instability and authoritarian rulers. In the 30 years that followed Ghana's independence, Africa saw some 70 separate coups. Typically, an initial coup set off several successive coups, each one making the transition to a permanent democratic government more difficult.

After seizing power, many military leaders not only eliminated their opponents but also, citing a need for security and stability, took advantage of emergency decrees to quash all forms of dissent. Under Africa's military regimes, civilians suffered a range of abuses.

In some African countries, coups brought to power and deposed leaders in rapid succession, producing continual political turmoil. In other countries, a strongman emerged who managed to consolidate his power and rule for an extended period.

**Mobutu Sese Seko, who ruled Zaire for more than three decades, ruthlessly suppressed opposition while amassing a huge personal fortune through corrupt means.**

Such was the case, for example, in Zaire, where Mobutu Sese Seko came to power in a 1965 military coup and remained in charge until 1997. Jean-Bédel Bokassa led the Central African Republic (which he renamed the Central African Empire) from 1966 to 1979. Francisco Macias Nguema of Equatorial Guinea held power for more than a decade (1968–1979); Idi Amin of Uganda, for eight years (1971–1979). Yet the longevity of these regimes did not translate into better conditions for citizens. In fact, all of these rulers were brutal dictators who gained reputations for massive human rights violations, including political killings and the widespread use of torture. Amin's regime, for instance, is believed to have been responsible for the deaths of as many as half a million Ugandans.

After independence, the ideal of multiparty democracy quickly withered throughout most of Africa. From the 1960s to the early 1990s, dozens of African countries had single-party political systems at least part of the time. In Algeria, for example, the National Liberation Front (FLN)—which was pivotal in the country's war for independence and has dominated politics since 1962—was the sole legal party between 1976 and 1989. In Ivory Coast, the Democratic Party of Côte d'Ivoire was the single legal political party from 1960 to 1990. Only the Democratic Party of Guinea was allowed in that West African nation in the years 1958–1984. Starting in 1969, Kenya had an unofficial single-party system under the ruling Kenya African National Union (KANU), and from 1982 to 1991 KANU's status as the country's lone legal party was official. As with dictatorships, single-party systems, by concentrating power and privilege, tend to lead to abuses. Such was the case in many African states.

## STRENGTHENING HUMAN RIGHTS PROTECTIONS

During the turbulent decades following decolonization, as human rights conditions in Africa remained poor—or, in some cases, deteriorated—the international community was developing a legal framework for rights protection. The International Convention on the Prevention and Punishment of the Crime of Genocide and the Convention Relating to the Status of Refugees—which entered into force in 1951 and 1954, respectively—were supplemented by the International Convention on the Elimination of All Forms of Racial Discrimination (1969), International Covenant on Civil and Political Rights (1976), International Covenant on Economic, Social and Cultural Rights (1976), Convention on the Elimination of All Forms of Discrimination Against Women (1981), Convention Against Torture and Other Cruel, Inhuman or Degrading Treatment or Punishment (1987), and Convention on the Rights of the Child (1990). In ratifying or acceding to these treaties—the steps differ but the result is the same—nations accepted a legal obligation to implement the rights contained in them. To monitor compliance, seven treaty bodies—each dealing with a specific human rights convention or covenant—were established. Composed of independent experts, the treaty bodies review the human rights reports each signatory nation must submit periodically, conduct inquiries when appropriate, and examine complaints of rights violations.

Like the United Nations, regional organizations also accepted responsibility for the promotion of human rights. For example, at the 1948 conference in Bogotá, Colombia, that resulted in the creation of the Organization of American States (OAS), nations of the Western Hemisphere promulgated the American Declaration of the Rights and Duties of Man. Eleven years later, in 1959, the OAS created the Inter-American Commission on Human Rights.

In the opinion of many experts, the Organization of African Unity (OAU)—Africa's first regional body—delayed making a commitment to human rights protection. Established in 1963, the OAU was preoccupied largely with eliminating the vestiges of colonialism and supporting the independence movements that were still active on the continent. In 1981, however, the OAU finally did lay the foundations for a regional rights system with the adoption of the African Charter on Human and

**African leaders at the opening session of the Organization of African Unity's 36th summit, July 2000. Although it adopted a human rights charter in 1981 and established a human rights commission five years later, the OAU made little tangible progress in improving fundamental rights and freedoms on the continent. The organization was replaced in 2002 by the African Union.**

Peoples' Rights. Many of the charter's provisions parallel the Universal Declaration of Human Rights. But, as might be surmised from the inclusion of "peoples' rights"—which include the rights of solidarity, group equality, and political and economic self-determination—the charter acknowledges the communal perspective that is highly valued in African cultures. The charter led to the formation, in 1986, of the African Commission on Human and Peoples' Rights. A continental monitoring group, the African Commission on Human and Peoples' Rights was given the responsibility of coordinating with national rights commissions and nongovernmental organizations (NGOs) to handle complaints of rights abuses; it was also charged with keeping the OAU apprised of the status of human rights throughout the continent.

Despite the formal commitments to human rights protection in Africa, abuses remained rampant. Many experts faulted the founding charter of the African Commission on Human and Peoples' Rights, which the scholar Obinna Okere characterized as "modest in its objectives and flexible in its means." National rights commissions also were ineffectual; co-opted by Africa's many dictators and ruling parties, they routinely turned a blind eye to the abuses they were supposed to address.

When a government is not committed to respecting human rights—or worse, when it systematically violates its citizens' rights in order to retain power—agreements, treaties, and rights commissions are meaningless. While democracy does not necessarily guarantee a government's respect for human rights, it at least provides a means of holding officials accountable for their actions and effecting change. Unfortunately, as late as 1989 there were only two African countries—Botswana and Mauritius—that Freedom House found were unencumbered by military control or one-party rule. Under these circumstances, leaders were unreceptive to calls for reform.

# GAINS AND SETBACKS

Three decades after the era of African independence began, the continent's journey to democracy remained decidedly unfinished. Thus a second revolution was inevitable. For many countries this revolution, which aimed to restore multiparty democracy, took place during the late 1980s and early 1990s. The gains were impressive. In 1989 all but two African countries were mired in dictatorship or single-party rule. By 1995, according to the British scholar John Wiseman, three out of four African countries boasted "competitive party systems."

Several factors, external as well as internal, help explain this sea change. By the late 1980s, the Cold War had wound down, and in 1991 the Soviet Union was officially dissolved. The end of the U.S.-Soviet struggle transformed international politics, with important consequences in Africa. The rationale for superpower support of warring parties on the continent—which had helped fuel much conflict—was removed. Also

gone was the incentive to funnel aid to a dictator or military regime merely to secure an ally.

Popular protests and a demand for democratic governance had helped the countries of Soviet-controlled Eastern Europe win their freedom. Inspired by this example, students, former leaders, rights advocates, and concerned citizens in several African countries joined mass demonstrations to speak out against government abuse and demand the end of single-party and military rule. The 1990 release of anti-apartheid leader Nelson Mandela, imprisoned in South Africa since 1962, also had tremendous symbolic importance. After decades of repression, the white-minority government of South Africa—arguably sub-Saharan Africa's most important country—was essentially conceding that it must reform. These developments seemed to portend an inexorable tide of reform across the continent.

## UNEVEN RESULTS

The spread of multiparty democracy in Africa during the 1990s did produce visible improvements in the promotion and protection of basic rights and freedoms. Across the continent, however, progress in human rights was uneven, in large measure because the commitment of individual governments to the democratic process varied.

In some countries, including Malawi, Mali, Benin, and Cape Verde, genuine and lasting reforms demonstrated a firm commitment to multiparty democracy. In these countries, improved human rights conditions were the rule.

Unfortunately, in many other countries democratic reforms proved short-lived, or the commitment to democracy was half-hearted from the outset. Elections do not necessarily a democracy make. Sociologist Marina Ottaway of the Carnegie Endowment for International Peace identified seven African countries (Burkina Faso, Cameroon, Ethiopia, Gabon, Guinea,

Mauritania, and Togo) where, between 1990 and 1995, "elections were seriously flawed." In still other countries, such as Kenya, elections were accompanied by widespread ethnic violence, deliberately stirred up by the government to intimidate and divide opposition voters.

During the 1990s Kenya amassed a shameful record of human rights violations, even after its transition to multiparty democracy. Arbitrary arrest, police brutality, torture, and unfair legal proceedings were especially common in the East African country. Similar abuses persisted in Nigeria, Africa's most populous country. While Kenya and Nigeria are certainly not the only African nations plagued by widespread human rights violations in an era of supposed reform, their cases are instructive.

## KENYA: HIDDEN ABUSES

A wildlife-rich, tourist-friendly country in East Africa, Kenya managed to conceal much of its torture and police-state activity under President Daniel arap Moi. In August 1978 Moi, then Kenya's vice president, assumed the presidency upon the death of President Jomo Kenyatta. A few months later, running unopposed, he was confirmed as president. While he claimed to be following in the footsteps of the beloved Kenyatta, Moi became increasingly repressive and authoritarian. By 1982 he declared KANU the country's only legal party. The following year and again in 1988, he was reelected to the presidency, running unopposed both times. But by the early 1990s, popular calls for reform compelled Moi to legalize opposition political parties once again. Still, he managed to win the multiparty elections of 1992 and 1997, in large part by exploiting ethnic divisions among opposition groups.

Throughout this time, violations of Kenyans' basic rights remained rampant. Some of the worst recorded abuse occurred in Nyayo House, a detention building located in the capital,

Kenyan president Daniel arap Moi acknowledges his supporters at an October 2001 rally in Nairobi. During his long rule (1978–2002), Moi used arbitrary detention and torture to silence his political opponents.

Nairobi. In his book *The New Africa*, Robert Press describes how Nyayo House prisoners charged with treason were beaten with whips, rubber tires, and timber.

These practices were not random cases of brutality, but rather natural extensions of Moi's authoritarian rule. A series of detention laws passed between 1982 and 1986 allowed the police to arrest and detain suspects arbitrarily. Many victims of this abuse were members of the outlawed organization Mwakenya. According to a 1998 report of the Kenya Human Rights Commission, more than 70 Mwakenya prisoners convicted in the late 1980s had no legal counsel, and most of their trials took place before their relatives or lawyers could be notified. Furthermore, the report said, all the prisoners showed signs of recent torture, and virtually all the convictions were founded on confessions. Even Gibson Kamau Kuria, a famous human rights lawyer, was detained immediately after he came forward to defend the Mwakenya suspects.

Kuria's campaign to free the Mwakenya prisoners made no headway, but a group called Release Political Prisoners (RPP) took up the cause. RPP members included mothers of the prisoners as well as high-profile supporters such as future Nobel Peace Prize winner Wangari Maathai.

In February 1992, RPP initiated a daytime hunger strike that would continue for a whole year. After police armed with clubs and tear gas dispersed the protesters from their site in front of

Nyayo House, RPP moved the operation to the basement of a nearby church. The ongoing hunger strikes eventually drew enough public exposure to convince the government to release all but 50 of the prisoners. However, though their release was a great victory, it did not mean the end of arbitrary detention and police torture in Kenya. According to a Kenya Human Rights Commission report from 1998, torture during that year was still "a standard procedure in police investigations."

By 2002, however, opposition groups were able to sweep KANU from power. Moi's successor, President Mwai Kibaki, finally began to lift the veil on police torture. The doors of Nyayo House were opened in 2003, and former prisoners were invited to speak to the public about the abuses they suffered there. Furthermore, as an expression of Kenya's new commitment to rights reform, President Kibaki appointed well-known human rights activists to his cabinet shortly after he entered office.

# NIGERIA: THE PERSISTENCE OF TORTURE

In Nigeria, a land of some 250 ethnic groups, independence in 1960 was followed by frequent coups and periods of military rule. A brief attempt at democracy during the early 1990s was cut short after the annulment of the 1993 presidential election. When the winner of that election, Moshood Abiola, declared himself the country's legitimate president, he was arrested. General Sani Abacha took power, ruling Nigeria with an iron hand. One of Abacha's most notorious acts was the 1995 execution of the famous playwright and environmentalist Ken Saro-Wiwa, along with eight other activists campaigning for economic justice for the Ogoni ethnic group. The executions drew international outrage and resulted in the European Union's imposition of economic sanctions on Nigeria, but this had no apparent effect on Abacha's ruthless rule.

In 1999, the year after the dictator's death, free elections brought Olusegun Obasanjo to the presidency. While President Obasanjo has managed to maintain civilian rule in Nigeria, and while he has won high marks from international observers for his efforts to resolve regional conflicts in Africa, in at least one respect his administration has been highly disappointing. Nigeria's human rights record remains almost as disturbing as it was under Sani Abacha and other military rulers.

A 2005 report by Human Rights Watch (HRW) exposed the gross violations of basic rights perpetrated by Nigeria's police and other law enforcement and security agencies. Arbitrary arrests, the report said, are common. So are due process violations such as failure to inform suspects of the reason for their arrest, extended pretrial detention, and the lack of legal representation. Most troubling, however, is the routine use of torture.

Olusegun Obasanjo, elected president of Nigeria in 1999, failed to dramatically improve his country's dismal human rights record.

Among police, the military, and law enforcement agencies, torture is seen as an acceptable tool. After years of human rights abuses at the hands of military rulers, even some of the victims of official torture regard it as inevitable, the HRW report says. "Of course the police will torture," a female detainee who had been viciously beaten while in detention in Lagos told HRW, "that is their work. If they see suspects, they must torture."

Victims of official torture in Nigeria are most often young men, but the elderly, women, and even children are not immune. Rape of female detainees is common.

Sometimes torture is used to extract confessions from criminal suspects, according to HRW, but other times it is used to punish members of political organizations, especially groups advocating more ethnic or regional autonomy.

# STRENGTHENING THE REGIONAL APPARATUS

Because widespread rights abuse in Africa has remained a constant throughout the postcolonial era, the need for an effective regional monitoring organization has always been clear. Ideally, national legal systems would handle all cases of rights violations. But many of them have had poor records—often because court systems lack independence from the political leaders responsible for the human rights violations in the first place.

The Organization of African Unity proved ineffectual in providing a regional human rights safety net. In 2002, however, the OAU became the African Union (AU), and observers have since noted a greater focus on human rights.

Perhaps the most significant regional development in human rights protection has been the establishment of the African Court on Human and Peoples' Rights (ACHPR). The ACHPR protocol came into force in January 2004; as of early 2006, judges had been elected though no cases had yet been heard. Unlike the regional human rights courts for Europe and the Americas, the ACHPR protocol permits actions to be brought on the basis of any human rights treaty or agreement ratified by the state in question (not only the African Charter). Furthermore, legal opinions may be solicited by any NGO recognized by the African Union. Thus the ACHPR has the potential to serve as a powerful instrument for promoting human rights and prosecuting violations.

The emergence of NGOs devoted to human rights in Africa, particularly since the late 1980s, is another positive trend. According to the research group Human Rights Internet, there are now more than 500 such NGOs in Africa. By investigating and publicizing abuses, these organizations can pressure governments to improve their human rights practices. And, in comparison with national rights commissions, they are more likely to remain independent and nonpartisan.

Despite these positive developments, and despite noticeable improvement in some African countries' records in recent years, the overall state of human rights on the continent continues to be poor. This has much to do with the quality of governance in Africa, because the primary responsibility for securing human rights lies with the individual state. The AU, the African Commission on Human and Peoples' Rights, and the ACHPR

The increasing number of nongovernmental organizations operating in Africa is seen as a positive development for long-term human rights prospects on the continent. Here a worker with Relief International, an American NGO, performs health screenings for Sudanese children displaced by the violence in Darfur.

can play a role in encouraging respect for fundamental rights and freedoms, but their efforts cannot be expected to yield dramatic results in the short term. Only better, more decent governance will lead reliably to greater respect for human rights, and that is a long-term proposition.

# THE ROLE OF THE INTERNATIONAL COMMUNITY

The international community also can play an important role in improving the human rights climate in Africa. Again, however, dramatic improvements are unlikely to be seen overnight. Although some rights advocates have said the international community is morally bound to use military intervention, if necessary, to stop an ongoing human rights disaster that rises to the level of genocide—as, perhaps, in Darfur—experience shows that such interventions will be very rare. And authoritarian regimes tend to be resistant, at least in the short term, to the remaining means of persuasion—moral, diplomatic, and economic pressure.

This is not to denigrate the use of such means to promote gradual improvement. In particular, the international community can use economic incentives—such as aid, debt relief, and trade opportunities—to reward governments that show progress in human rights and to encourage governments with spotty records to improve.

However, some scholars assert that the international community must do much more. According to World Bank statistics for 2004, Africa is home to 23 of the 25 poorest countries in the world (as measured by gross national income per capita); an estimated 46 percent of all people in sub-Saharan Africa survive on less than $1 per day. "The vast majority of our people are . . . facing the struggle for existence in its brutal immediacy," argues Nigerian scholar Claude Ake. "Theirs is a totally consuming struggle." Claiming that development is a "third-generation" human right,

# FAILING TO ABOLISH SLAVERY

One of Africa's most long-standing types of abuse, slavery on the continent may date back (at least in some form) to the third millenium B.C. in ancient Egypt. It is a tradition that Arabs, Europeans, and peoples of the Americas once played a part in. The transatlantic slave trade, which occurred between the 16th and 19th centuries, was perhaps the darkest chapter in the history of slavery. Since that period, internal trading in Africa has dramatically declined. Yet slavery has survived intact in pockets of the continent, including the northern countries of Mauritania and Sudan. International and regional rights monitors have had little success in dismantling these slave systems.

People in these countries may become indentured for a number of reasons: dire poverty puts them at the mercy of a class of exploiters; they belong to an ethnic group that another people has subjugated; or they are victim to old cultural traditions that have not yet been abolished, such as the practice of placing West African girls in the servitude of village priests.

Mauritania and Sudan both have ethnically based slave systems, composed of Arab masters and black African slaves. The central difference between the two systems is that Mauritanian slaves are born into an 800-year-old tradition, while Sudanese victims typically become slaves through abduction. In Mauritania the majority of slaves (who number between 100,000 and 1 million, according to different estimates) inherit their slave status from their parents.

Most of Sudan's slaves—estimated to number around 100,000 by the American Anti-Slavery Group (AASG)—have been abducted through raids that the government is believed to have endorsed. The militiamen who have raided in Darfur and southern Sudan receive no pay from the government, so they often support themselves through looting and slave abduction.

some critics suggest that rich nations are obligated to assist impoverished Africa as a matter of human rights.

But there is also a more subtle argument. While not a cause of (and certainly not an excuse for) human rights abuse, poverty is often associated with less rigorous adherence to human rights standards. A more prosperous citizenry—which will tend to be better educated, have more access to information, and have a greater sense of empowerment—is more likely to hold its government accountable for the government's human rights

Concerned groups have found practical ways to combat slavery in these two countries. In the case of Sudan, some villages vulnerable to raids have enjoyed the protection of rebel armies. Another obvious weapon in the fight against slavery is simply to expose the issue to the world. This certainly has been lacking in Mauritania. Although slavery has been abolished under national law since 1980, Mauritanian slaveholders continue to flout the law.

Nongovernmental organizations that work to emancipate slaves go a step beyond exposing the victims' suffering. In Sudan, Western humanitarian agencies have coordinated with local groups to establish an "Underground Railroad" of secret routes and hideouts for fugitive slaves.

One highly controversial component of this effort in Sudan is the slave redemption program. Orchestrated chiefly by the Swiss group Christian Solidarity International and supported by the AASG, this program employs local Sudanese to find enslaved individuals and purchase their freedom from their masters. Christian Solidarity International reports that it has negotiated for the freedom of 80,000 Sudanese and provided aid for them. However, opponents of this practice—and there are many—argue that it fails to address the root of the problem, and even increases the problem. Individuals like Jim Jacobson, president of Christian Freedom International (CFI), have dropped their support for the redemption program because they believe it bolsters slave demand. "[W]hile we have undoubtedly freed some slaves, we are even now creating incentives to take slaves," he says.

Anti-redemption organizations like CFI remain committed to all underground efforts that do not entail the purchase of slaves. Many of the slaves who successfully escape end up in Egypt, where they may apply for refugee status with the United Nations High Commissioner for Refugees.

performance. So by alleviating poverty in Africa, the international community can help create a political climate that is more conducive to respect for fundamental rights and freedoms. One difficulty lies in ensuring that economic aid reaches the people for which it is intended: historically, many of Africa's corrupt rulers have managed to siphon off aid money for their personal use.

# 4 SEGREGATION IN SOUTHERN AFRICA

In the campaign for human rights in Africa, the peoples of southern Africa stand apart. Long after other African countries began wrestling with the new challenges of independence, Zimbabwe and South Africa remained crippled by governments run solely by whites. The black majorities of these countries, and the Indians and people of mixed race situated just above them in the social hierarchy, were by law subordinate to a white minority composed of people of British and Dutch descent. By no means were Zimbabwe and South Africa the only African countries with long-standing human rights problems, yet nowhere else during the post-colonial era were a majority of blacks denied basic freedoms for such an extended period.

In South Africa, the system that ensured blacks did not have fundamental rights was known as apartheid, which in the settler language of Afrikaans means "separateness." Apartheid aimed to segregate the races in all spheres of private and public life, in the process

disenfranchising the black population. A similar system of segregation was implemented in Rhodesia (the former name of Zimbabwe). Throughout much of the 20th century the African National Congress (ANC) in South Africa and various nationalist groups in Rhodesia waged a resistance campaign against their countries' regimes. Government clampdowns on the resistance were brutally effective, however.

The white regime of Rhodesia, which was a British colony until it declared independence in 1965, finally collapsed in 1980 after prolonged economic sanctions and a lengthy civil war. However, the end of white rule in Zimbabwe did not usher in the kind of democracy that people hoped for, nor did it lead to the protection of basic rights. In the eyes of the international community, much of the blame for Zimbabwe's troubles rests with dictator Robert Mugabe, the former rebel leader who has stretched out his reign since 1980. One of the longest-serving presidents in Africa, Mugabe has robbed many Zimbabweans of the very freedoms they fought so hard for.

Nearly the opposite scenario has played out in South Africa, which passed through its own difficult transition to demonstrate what real democratic change can achieve in government and civil society. Its new constitution, adopted in 1996, is cited as one of the most progressive in the field of human rights protection, and the number of NGOs devoted to general human rights concerns in South Africa is nearly double the number of similar groups in any other African country.

## THE FOUNDATIONS OF SEGREGATION

Apartheid was not officially introduced in South Africa until 1948, yet it was the culmination of a legislative process that the government began in the early 20th century. Similarly, Rhodesia's segregationist plan had roots that reached far back in the colonial era.

One of the oldest forms of discrimination in southern Africa prescribed where blacks and other nonwhites could live. In 1913 the South African parliament passed the Natives Land Act, which limited blacks to purchasing and owning land that fell within the boundaries of government-designated reserves. A subsequent act in 1936 further spelled out the land restrictions on blacks. Rhodesia's land legislation also reserved huge shares of land for the country's white minority, which made up a mere 2 percent of the population.

In South Africa, the Urban Areas Act of 1923 restricted blacks from living in the country's cities. The Group Areas Act, passed in 1950 along with several other apartheid laws, further delineated where blacks could live. It effectively established "homelands" for South Africa's blacks. Dubbed "the very essence of apartheid" by Daniel Malan, then South Africa's prime minister, the Group Areas Act authorized the government to uproot and transfer entire communities in order to create white residential zones.

Soon black South Africans were restricted in where they could go as well as where they could live. The Population Registration Act, passed in the same year as the Group Areas Act, required individuals to register their ethnic identity with the government. Rights protection, educational opportunities, and economic standing were largely determined by how one was registered. Blacks who wished to go to a white area needed to present passes, and those caught without the correct documents faced fines and other penalties. Rhodesia's Native Regulations Act similarly placed obstructions on the free movement of blacks. People who failed to present identity papers could even be jailed or placed in labor camps.

The governments of South Africa and Rhodesia recognized that they could retain power only by excluding most of the populace from the political process. To that end, South Africa passed, in 1950, the Suppression of Communism Act, which purported to target only Communists. In fact, under the act's broad language, a large number of dissidents—including those advocating full rights for blacks—were banned from meeting with one another and from making public appearances. Lawyer and activist Nelson Mandela, whom the government identified as a threat shortly after he helped form the ANC Youth League in 1944, labored under a political ban throughout most of the 1950s. The ANC, whose demonstration campaign had stirred unrest by decade's end, was banned as well. Four years later, Rhodesia's foremost nationalist groups, the Zimbabwe African National Union (ZANU) and Zimbabwe African People's Union (ZAPU), were also banned.

South African lawmakers often dressed up apartheid legislation to give the impression that it met the specific needs of

In this photograph from the 1950s, African National Congress supporters gather for a rally as part of a civil disobedience campaign. In 1960 the South African government outlawed the ANC.

blacks. One such act was the Bantu Education Act of 1953 ("Bantu" was used as the general term for blacks in South Africa); it established how the black homelands' schools were administered and what was taught.

The Promotion of Bantu Self-Government Act (1959) also purported to "accommodate" ethnic groups by establishing boundaries for them and letting them exercise some political rights, albeit under rigid conditions. Nonwhites elected traditional leaders of the 10 established homelands, whose boundaries were drawn to represent 10 different nations. Under this power arrangement, the traditional leaders could lead their people, but the people still did not enjoy the rights of full-fledged citizens. The true purpose of the homeland system was not to preserve traditional South African culture but, as Nelson Mandela observed, "to preserve the status quo where three million whites owned 87 percent of the land, and relegate the eight million Africans to the remaining 13 percent."

From the 1960s until the end of white rule in southern Africa, the conflict between the governments and the resistance movements only became more violent. South Africa declared a state of emergency after the Sharpeville massacre in March 1960, in which 69 demonstrators were killed; some had been shot in the back as they were running away from approaching police officers. In Rhodesia, Prime Minister Ian Smith declared a state of emergency shortly after signing the Unilateral Declaration of Independence for Rhodesia in 1965.

Bodies litter the ground in the aftermath of the Sharpeville massacre. On March 21, 1960, South African police opened fire on a crowd of unarmed black demonstrators, killing 69 and wounding at least 180. The demonstrators were protesting South Africa's pass laws, which restricted the freedom of movement of black citizens.

The Ninety-Day Detention Law, passed in 1963, initiated an era of state-sanctioned violence against South Africans. The police were given the go-ahead to abuse and torture prisoners as they saw fit, using brutal tactics like suffocation and electric shock. Many South Africans died while in police custody during this period. The Sabotage Act, passed in the same year, expanded the legal definition of sabotage. This law helped empower the prosecution against ANC leaders in the Rivonia Trial of 1963–1964, a famous court case that ended in life imprisonment sentences for Nelson Mandela and other ANC leaders. The same year that Mandela was convicted, Robert Mugabe and another Zimbabwean resistance leader, Joshua Nkomo, were imprisoned, but the two leaders would be freed in 1974, 16 years before Mandela's release.

## TEARING DOWN THE SYSTEM

Apartheid proved to be more firmly entrenched in South Africa than segregation was in Zimbabwe. The Rhodesian government did not have the resources of South Africa's regime, including its formidable security force. The fight for democracy in South Africa stands as one of the continent's most inspiring and successful crusades for human rights.

The ANC, which was founded in 1912, was the foremost anti-apartheid organization. Nelson Mandela joined in 1943 as he was embarking on a career in law. The following year Mandela, his friend Walter Sisulu, and future law partner Oliver Tambo founded the ANC Youth League in the hopes of pushing the anti-apartheid movement forward. To that end, leaders drew up what was called the Plan of Action in response to the new apartheid measures initiated in 1948. The plan, implemented in 1949, included strikes, boycotts, and other forms of nonviolent resistance.

The Plan of Action paved the way, in 1952, for the ANC's Defiance Campaign, another series of protests conducted after

Prime Minister Malan rejected the ANC's pleas for basic rights. The Defiance Campaign was highly organized. While it did not force the repeal of apartheid legislation, it did expose people to the ANC agenda and inspired more blacks to get involved at the grassroots level. The organization's membership grew from 20,000 to 100,000 in 1952 alone. In addition, the ANC followed through on its commitment to national unity by coordinating the protests with the South African Indian Congress (SAIC). The same desire for unity later inspired the creation of the Congress Alliance, an anti-apartheid coalition that included the ANC, the SAIC, the Congress of Democrats (COD), and the Colored People's Congress (CPC). In 1955 the Congress Alliance adopted the Freedom Charter, a landmark document that contained a long list of basic rights that the apartheid regime was being petitioned to address.

In 1962 Mandela was given a five-year prison sentence for illegally exiting the country and inciting others to strike. The following year, the sentence was interrupted so that Mandela, Walter Sisulu, and nine others could stand trial for the much more serious charge of sabotage. Mandela used the opportunity at the opening of the defense case to deliver one of his most famous public statements. "I have cherished the ideal of a democratic and free society in which all persons live together in harmony and with equal opportunities," he said. "It is an ideal which I hope to live for and achieve. But, if needs be, it is an ideal for which I am prepared to die."

Mandela and the others avoided the death penalty but received life sentences, a large chunk of which they spent on Robben Island, a prison infamous for the brutal conditions to which inmates were subjected. Mandela's imprisonment stirred the ire of the international community, which until then had hesitated to take action against apartheid. In the decades after the leader's sentence, the world's developed nations answered

Nelson Mandela (left) and Walter Sisulu in the prison yard at Robben Island, 1965. The previous year, the two ANC leaders had received life sentences at the infamous Rivonia Trial.

the UN's call to impose diplomatic and economic sanctions on South Africa. In 1974 the UN expelled South Africa from the General Assembly, and over the following years the South African regime became progressively more isolated from the world community. By the end of the 1980s, economic sanctions—particularly those imposed by the United States and the United Kingdom—began to take a heavy toll. The South African government began considering compromise agreements with the ANC so that its most illustrious leader could finally be released from jail.

# THE DEATH KNELL OF MINORITY RULE

Like South African leaders, Rhodesia's Ian Smith believed that white rule could withstand all the campaigns to end it, which included crippling trade sanctions. In 1969 the prime minister

## HUMAN RIGHTS IN THE COURTROOM

When he faced charges of illegally inciting people to strike and leaving the country without a passport, Nelson Mandela went to trial in 1962 as a seasoned lawyer. Providing his own defense, he argued during the first court statement of the trial, "I would say that the whole life of any thinking African in this country drives him continuously to a conflict between his conscience on the one hand and the law on the other." Mandela's defense of his actions did not save him from a five-year prison sentence, but he did expose the world to the dilemma faced by so many conscientious lawyers in Africa. Before and after Mandela, attorneys in Africa have often had to fight for justice in an unjust system.

Since Mandela's first courtroom stand, African lawyers have gained ground in the field of civil rights protection. The democratic reforms of some countries have created safeguards that are effective, as long as lawyers have the means and the desire to protect their clients' rights. Such is the mission of Gibson Kamau Kuria, a Kenyan lawyer who uses constitutional law as his most potent weapon. "Kuria," the author Robert Press observes, "does what infuriates any egotistical political leader who would trample on those rights—he cites the law."

However, in countries where many unjust laws remain unchanged, human rights lawyers have often waged an impossible battle. When, for example, Nigerian activist Ken Saro-Wiwa and his associates were charged with the murder of four Ogoni chiefs in a hasty trial marred by gross injustice, the defense team withdrew in protest. The lawyers concluded that mounting a defense in a trial whose outcome was clearly predetermined would only lend legitimacy to the proceedings.

But as Mandela did when anticipating his sentence, Saro-Wiwa testified in the name of justice so that other human rights activists would take up the fight after his conviction. "I and my colleagues are not the only ones on trial," he told the judge. "We all stand on trial, my lord, for by our actions we have denigrated our country and jeopardized the future of our children."

claimed that the new Rhodesian constitution "sounded the death knell of the notion of majority rule" and "would entrench government in the hands of civilized [white] Rhodesians for all time." However, under continuing international pressure, Smith finally began making concessions in 1978. The year after an aborted transition to power in 1979, in which a compromise agreement secured only 28 of 100 parliamentary seats for black members, Robert Mugabe's ZANU Party won the majority. In the reconstituted parliament of the newly renamed Zimbabwe, black members claimed 80 of the seats.

Before becoming prime minister, Mugabe had gained the support of many people who were won over by his pledges of democracy and racial reconciliation. The new constitution's Declaration of Rights promised the restoration of personal freedoms. Furthermore, the inclusion of ZAPU party leader Joshua Nkomo in Mugabe's cabinet seemed to signal reconciliation between ZAPU and ZANU, which had suffered serious fallouts during the civil war.

Early on, however, Mugabe proved willing to sacrifice human rights for the sake of holding onto power. In 1982, claiming that his former associate Nkomo was plotting a coup, Mugabe effectively expelled ZAPU from Parliament and launched a military assault in the Matabeland region, where Nkomo and ZAPU drew their main support from ethnic Ndebele people. Thousands of innocent Ndebele civilians were slaughtered, many by the prime minister's notorious Fifth Brigade.

Another of Mugabe's major failures has been his mishandling of the land redistribution process. At the time he gained power, a small minority of white farmers owned most of the country's land, and while it was grossly unfair that the majority of native Zimbabweans did not enjoy equal opportunity as landowners, it was still essential that the redistribution program follow due process and respect the rights of all Zimbabwean citizens, white and black. As a demonstration of goodwill to white farmers, Mugabe initially declared that the government would not take land from anyone who had a legal claim to it.

The Land Acquisition Act, passed in 1992, proposed a feasible solution to the redistribution question. This measure instituted a government program to purchase land from white farmers and dole it out to the landless black majority. However, Mugabe soon went back on his promise to respect due process for white farmers, and in a September 1993 speech he described how the land program would really be implemented. "If white settlers just took the land from us without paying for it," he said, "we can, in a similar way, just

Robert Mugabe led Zimbabwe to independence in 1980, but over the course of more than 25 years in power, he became one of Africa's most corrupt and despotic rulers.

take it from them without paying for it." By 2000 Mugabe had begun what he called "fast-track land reform," effectively giving war veterans and high-level ZANU members clearance to forcibly take white-owned plantations. During the subsequent land grab, the government made little effort to ensure the safety of white farmers. Several murders were committed, and the government failed to investigate these crimes.

For some time opposition has grown to Mugabe's abuses and destructive policies. A strong resistance campaign led by the

Movement for Democratic Change (MDC) has been ongoing since the organization formed in 1999. However, Mugabe has used a variety of illicit means—including detainment and torture of political opponents, press censorship, voter intimidation, electoral fraud, and even the misappropriation of food aid—to maintain his grip on power. Ending his long reign, and the human rights abuses that have accompanied it, promises to be a difficult task.

## A DIFFERENT PATH

Majority rule took considerably longer to reach South Africa than Zimbabwe. But the ANC leadership, unlike Robert Mugabe, has managed to remain faithful to its original goals. Beginning in the mid-1980s, several events signaled the inevitable demise of apartheid. In 1986, for example, South Africa's identity-pass laws were repealed. Four years later, in 1990, the government lifted the ban on the ANC, and Nelson Mandela was released from prison after 27 long years.

Yet the transition to democracy came neither smoothly nor immediately after this milestone. Several years of sometimes contentious negotiations between the government of President F. W. de Klerk and Mandela and the ANC preceded South Africa's first free elections. And during this time, South Africa was convulsed by intense violence, some perpetrated by the security forces against blacks, some committed by blacks against other blacks. As the talks progressed, however, the violence finally subsided, and in 1993 delegates agreed on an interim constitution. In free, nonracial elections held the following year, Nelson Mandela and the ANC claimed a landslide victory.

The first major task of the new administration was setting up the Truth and Reconciliation Commission (TRC), which was followed by the drafting of a new constitution. The TRC was a government-sponsored endeavor to establish a complete histori-

**A young South African displays an election poster for Nelson Mandela, 1994. Mandela won the country's first nonracial presidential elections in a landslide.**

cal account of the apartheid years and, whenever feasible, to reconcile the oppressors and the victims. The next project was the introduction of the new constitution in 1996. It included an exhaustive Bill of Rights that recognized once-neglected rights such as those to fair labor practices, health and social services, and a basic education. As the document promised, this list of rights has since stood as "a cornerstone of democracy"—and as a hopeful example of the type of rights reform that is achievable in Africa.

# WOMEN AND CHILDREN: AFRICA'S MOST VULNERABLE

**A**lthough human rights violations affect Africans of all backgrounds, women and children are particularly at risk. Gender-biased property inheritance and divorce laws, which exist in various African countries, result in a lower standard of living for many African women. Rates of rape and HIV/AIDS infection among African women, as well as abduction and forced military recruitment among children, have risen in recent years. These trends make it clear that Africa's women and children are in need of more protection.

At the most basic level, the large majority of African governments have at least recognized the need to protect the rights of women and children. All African countries except Somalia have ratified the UN convention regarding children, and all except Somalia and Sudan have ratified the convention on women. These documents are known, respectively, as the Convention on the Rights of the Child and the Convention on the Elimination of All Forms of Discrimination

Against Women (CEDAW). Described as the International Bill of Rights for Women, CEDAW sets forward many of the rights that previous conventions failed to state explicitly, namely the rights of women to vote; own property or business ventures; choose a marriage partner or file for divorce; and have access to health services, education, training, or gainful employment.

The advancement of African women's rights has been slow since CEDAW came into force in 1981. Recognizing the lack of progress, the African Commission on Human and Peoples' Rights established a separate protocol to the African Charter in 2003. Although the African Charter identifies the need to protect women from discrimination, it fails to describe in detail the many forms discrimination can take. The women's rights protocol is more descriptive and includes, for example, articles guaranteeing women the right to control their own fertility, including the right to decide whether to have children (and how many) and the right to use contraception; equal rights with men in marriage and in the event of a marriage's dissolution, including the right to an equitable distribution of joint property; and equal employment opportunities as men, along with equal pay for the same work. The Protocol on the Rights of Women in Africa came into force in November 2005. As of April 2006, 17 countries had ratified the protocol.

# PROTECTING WOMEN FROM PHYSICAL HARM

Complete gender equality is an elusive goal, but stopping the most serious abuses against women, including acts that inflict serious physical harm, must clearly take priority. Two of the most horrific and common manifestations of physical abuse against African women are rape and genital mutilation.

Rape is common in nearly all armed conflicts in Africa. Between 1994 and 2004 there were a staggering number of rapes

**These African Union peacekeepers have taken up positions near a displaced persons camp in Darfur in an effort to prevent the rape of women who venture outside the camp to gather firewood. In Darfur, as in other African conflict zones, rape has been used as a weapon by the warring parties.**

throughout the continent, owing greatly to the chaos of conflict in Rwanda, Burundi, the Democratic Republic of the Congo, and Sudan. A BBC news article in February 2005 reported that an estimated 25,000 girls and women were raped during the 1994 genocide in Rwanda. It may be some time before experts reach an accurate figure on how many girls and women have been raped in Sudan. According to eyewitness reports, victims have been as young as eight. Even females who have successfully reached displacement camps are not safe, as attacks have been reported on women who ventured outside of camps to get water or firewood.

The psychological and physical effects of rape on women can be devastating. In cases of gang rape, women suffer wounds that may never heal, and the chances of contracting HIV/AIDS are greatly increased. The social life of victimized women may also suffer in communities where rape is a source of shame. In some cultures, it is justified for a husband to divorce a wife who has been raped, which often leaves her to scramble for a means of support.

Obviously, rape cannot be eliminated entirely—in Africa or the rest of the world. Curtailing the high incidence rate is possible, however, particularly if leaders work to establish peace in Africa's most war-torn countries. In addition, regional and international authorities can continually send out the signal to combatants that all rape offenders will be held accountable. The International Criminal Court and other tribunals have publicized this message

A traumatized woman describes to a health care worker her gang rape at the hands of soldiers, Kanyabayonga, Democratic Republic of the Congo, 2006. In addition to the usual psychological and physical harm suffered by women who have been sexually violated, rape victims in Africa are likely to be stigmatized by society. Some African cultures consider it warranted for a husband to divorce his wife if she has been raped.

by including rape as a possible charge. Under particular circumstances, rape may be prosecuted as an instrument of genocide and a crime against humanity. The women's rights protocol to the African Charter also classifies rape as a war crime under certain conditions.

If rape is universally acknowledged as an offense against women, that is not the case with female genital mutilation (FGM), a set of rituals traditionally practiced in 28 African countries. Although there is growing consensus among rights advocates and the international community that the continued existence of FGM is a human rights issue, African groups who still perform FGM regard it as a cultural practice. And, it must be noted, developing nations have sometimes accused the West of attempting to impose its cultural values on the rest of the world in the guise of promoting so-called universal human rights.

FGM, which practitioners believe maintains the purity of girls and women, involves the removal of part or all of the female genitalia. Fourteen African countries have enacted laws making FGM a criminal offense, but the procedure continues to be widely practiced throughout the continent. The World Health Organization reports that every year 2 million more girls are forced to undergo FGM, joining the 100 to 140 million females who already have endured the procedure. Amnesty International estimates that FGM is performed on one-half or more of the women and girls in as many as 19 African countries. Rates are especially high in Djibouti (90–98 percent), Egypt (97 percent), Eritrea (90 percent), Ethiopia (90 percent), Mali (90–94 percent), and Somalia (98 percent).

Because FGM is a form of mutilation, the physical impact is permanent. Compounding the horror is the fact that the procedure is often performed with crude and unsanitary instruments, without anesthesia, and by persons with no medical training

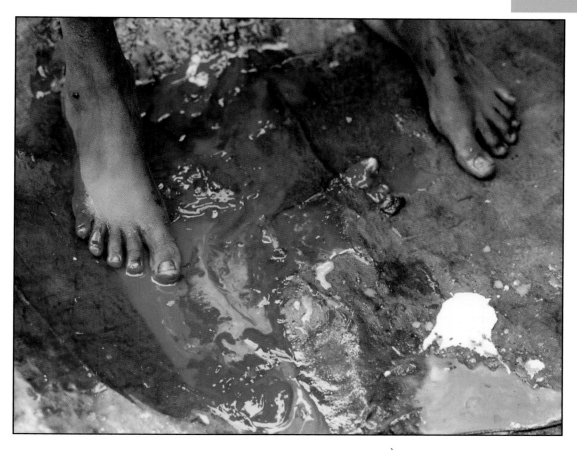

A 16-year-old Kenyan stands in a pool of her own blood after undergoing female circumcision, also known as female genital mutilation, or FGM. Fourteen African countries have enacted laws criminalizing FGM, but the practice continues.

(typically family members or friends). The pain can be unbearable, and the risk of death is very real. Many victims suffer severe psychological trauma. Others contract HIV/AIDS or other forms of infection due to open wounds or unclean instruments.

Few people have been convicted of practicing FGM. Even where there are laws against it, many law enforcement agencies still hesitate to prosecute because they do not wish to intrude on traditions performed within the home or the community. Experts believe that education programs about FGM-associated health problems could diminish the practice.

# CHILDREN

The prevalence of HIV/AIDS, poverty, and armed conflict in Africa has had a horrific impact on the children. The escalating rate of HIV/AIDS, particularly in southern Africa, has orphaned millions of children who are left with limited means. In times of hopeless poverty and war, children are more susceptible to terrible labor conditions and slave abduction. Wars have also led to the widespread recruitment of child soldiers in West and Central Africa, as well as in Angola, Sudan, and Somalia.

Every year, according to the United Nations, at least 200,000 children are ushered into the slave trade in West and Central Africa. Unlike the slave systems that are founded on raiding in Sudan or chattel slavery in Mauritania, child slavery is usually based on deception. Individuals known as traffickers approach desperately poor families and, claiming that they have jobs for children, offer the parents a meager sum if they agree to let the children take those jobs (which are typically said to be a considerable distance away). Recognizing that they cannot provide for their children, and hoping that employment will offer the youngsters the prospect for a better life, many poor parents agree. But when the children are taken away, often to a neighboring country, they never receive the pay that was promised. Instead, they are forced to work indefinitely—typically under conditions that approach slave labor—until they have paid off their supposed "debt" to the trafficker. These children are often forced into prostitution or become victims of sexual abuse.

Perhaps the most effective weapon against child slavery is to expose trafficking operations. When, for example, a slave boat is apprehended and the story appears in the international media or in human rights reports, leaders typically place pressure on African governments. Legislators have responded to this pressure by passing national laws that give teeth to international and

As a child, this young woman was abducted by Ugandan rebels of the Lord's Resistance Army, who cut off her ears, nose, and lips. Africa's many civil wars have contributed to the widespread abuse and brutalization of children.

regional conventions against trafficking. In Benin, for example, a law requires adults to present a certificate when they travel with children outside the country, and neighboring countries have enacted similar laws. Time will tell whether West African governments will more effectively enforce these laws in the future.

Many children who are abducted end up as fighters for government or rebel armies. Other children volunteer or are coerced into fighting. Those who volunteer most often come from war-torn areas where joining an army may be a way to escape dire conditions, win peer respect, or avenge the murder of a family member.

There are more child soldiers in Africa than in any other continent. The Coalition to Stop the Use of Child Soldiers estimated that up to 100,000 African child soldiers were involved in a conflict in mid-2004. The large majority of countries with child soldiers are located in West and Central Africa, though in 2004 Sudan recorded as many as 17,000 child soldiers in its rebel armies and government militias. Groups devoted to rescuing these children, like Save the Children and UNICEF, coordinate with militia and government groups to demobilize child soldiers and reintegrate them into society.

Three other countries with massive numbers of child fighters are Ivory Coast (also called Côte d'Ivoire), the Democratic Republic of the Congo (DRC), and Uganda. According to a May 2003 report by Integrated Regional Information Networks (IRIN), a humanitarian news resource, more than 9,000 children were taken from the Liberian refugee population to fight in Ivory Coast. Some boys were as young as eight. The same source reported a total of 30,000 child soldiers in the DRC in 2003. Many of these soldiers were girls who joined to escape servitude

China Keitetsi holds a copy of her memoir, *The Little Girl with the Kalashnikov*. As a nine-year-old in Uganda, Keitetsi was forced to fight in the National Resistance Army. Today she is a spokeswoman for UNICEF on the plight of child soldiers, as many as 100,000 of whom may be fighting in African conflicts, according to a recent estimate.

or other abuse they faced at home. These girls are often used as porters, carrying heavy munitions or other supplies for the warring groups. They are very vulnerable to sexual abuse.

The Lord's Resistance Army (LRA), a rebel group that has ravaged northern Uganda since 1986, is notorious for kidnapping children and making them soldiers. The Global Internally Displaced People Project has received estimates that abducted children make up 80 percent of the LRA, and that since the LRA insurgency began, more than 28,000 children have been abducted. The LRA takes a majority of these child soldiers by raiding displacement camps. The only defense against raids for people in camps and villages is to evade them. In the evenings, thousands of Ugandan children, known as night commuters, have regularly fled the countryside for the protection of the cities.

Along with war crimes and crimes against humanity, the International Criminal Court lists the recruitment of children under 15 years as a crime under its jurisdiction. In 2003 the prosecutor for the Special Court for Sierra Leone, which was set up in 2002 by the United Nations in conjunction with the national government, issued charges against soldiers who "conscripted, enlisted or used" children under 15 to fight.

Since 2002 the newly formed African Committee on the Rights and Welfare of the Child has met regularly to discuss the abuses that particularly affect African children. The committee grew out of the African Commission's Charter on the Rights and Welfare of the Child, passed in 1990 as a regional complement to the UN Convention on the Rights of the Child. Thus far, the committee has addressed the various effects of armed conflict and HIV/AIDS on children.

## HIV/AIDS-RELATED ABUSES

Social evils such as mass rape, slavery, exploitation, and discrimination appear even worse in light of how they all help spread

HIV/AIDS. Such violations have been termed HIV/AIDS–related abuses, which rights advocates say have been neglected too long. Women and children, particularly girls, bear the brunt of these abuses. According to Stephen Lewis, the UN Secretary-General's Special Envoy on HIV/AIDS in Africa, "The toll [of AIDS] on women and girls is beyond human imagining."

A 2004 report by UNAIDS (the Joint United Nations Programme on HIV/AIDS) estimated that women and girls make up almost 57 percent of all people infected with HIV in sub-Saharan Africa, and females make up a staggering 76 percent of HIV-infected young people (ages 15–24). The clear disparity between the HIV rate among females and among males is most evident in the southern African nations of South Africa, Zambia, and Zimbabwe, where young women between 15 and 24 years old are three to six times more likely to be infected than young men. Females also are especially vulnerable in Sierra Leone, Togo, DRC, and Uganda. This crisis facing African women and children is compounded by the fact that post-exposure prophylaxis (PEP)—emergency medication used to protect people exposed to HIV—is not yet widely available to rape victims.

Human rights abuse and neglect creates a vicious cycle that perpetuates the spread of HIV/AIDS among females in Africa. The cycle may begin when an evil like rape escalates the risk of contracting HIV; then the majority of the women who become infected are not provided access to affordable medication and consequently die much sooner than they otherwise would. The deceased mothers may leave behind daughters who lack the basic necessities, and to get by, those girls may eventually consider prostitution or other practices where the risk of HIV contraction is high. The cycle is thus perpetuated.

Unequal property and inheritance laws and customs—which are still prevalent throughout much of sub-Saharan Africa—also

# AIDS AND HUMAN RIGHTS

In raising awareness of the women and children suffering from HIV/AIDS, advocates never wish to downplay how all infected people suffer. One of the many common obstacles that both male and female patients face is the lack of affordable antiretroviral (ARV) drugs, which do not cure HIV but greatly lessen symptoms for extended periods. According to UNAIDS, of the estimated 25 million adults and children in sub-Saharan Africa with HIV/AIDS at the end of 2004, only a fraction had access to ARV drugs.

One factor that has impeded the availability is the high price tag of patented drugs. For some time, global ARV manufacturers like GlaxoSmithKline guarded their patents, preventing other companies from producing low-cost generic versions. Advocates eventually came forward to assert that the desire to maintain profits should not violate the rights of the impoverished millions who simply wish to live longer. Groups like the World Trade Organization (WTO) and UNAIDS have acknowledged access to ARV drugs as a fundamental right. The Doha Declaration, signed by the WTO's 142 member states in 2001, announced that governments must henceforth relax patent protection in cases of national health emergency.

Today, drug companies in Africa are making generic versions of ARVs under less stringent patents. There are manufacturing operations in South Africa and Kenya, which are increasing the availability of the drugs for ARV programs in Mozambique, Uganda, and Tanzania. Of course, the success of drug programs largely rests on how dedicated national governments are to stamping out AIDS. Leading that mission is the government of Botswana, which has promised to foot the bill for any HIV/AIDS patient seeking antiretroviral medication.

perpetuate the spread of HIV/AIDS. In some places, for example, a wife cannot inherit her deceased husband's property, which goes instead to his family. Similarly, in the event of divorce, the man often retains all property. Thus a woman may suddenly find herself destitute and homeless. With few options, she may be forced into prostitution to support herself, which increases dramatically the risk of contracting HIV/AIDS.

Unequal property and inheritance laws, then, do not just discriminate against women but also put them in circumstances

A nurse at the Aidchild Orphanage in Uganda's Mpigi district sorts antiretroviral medications, 2005. According to UN estimates, more than 12 million children in sub-Saharan Africa have been orphaned by HIV/AIDS. Lacking the means to support themselves, many are particularly vulnerable to exploitation.

where their health is in jeopardy. Likewise, rape and war do not stand alone as evils in themselves; they are also contributing factors to the spread of HIV/AIDS and to the rise of child conscription. However, the converse is also true: the reduction of HIV infection and child conscription is possible through effective health programs and peacekeeping efforts.

 **GENOCIDE**

In the wake of the Holocaust, during which 6 million European Jews and others were murdered by the Nazi regime of Germany, the states of the newly formed UN General Assembly adopted the International Convention on the Prevention and Punishment of the Crime of Genocide (1948). The agreement was essentially a promise by signatory nations that never again would genocide be allowed to happen.

In the ensuing decades, however, that pledge would strike many people as rather hollow. Between 1975 and 1979, the world stood by as the regime of Pol Pot systematically killed an estimated 2 million people in Cambodia. The international community also failed to take concerted action to stop the "ethnic cleansing" campaign in Bosnia-Herzegovina between 1992 and 1995; that genocide claimed some 200,000 victims. And in 1994 the world watched as an estimated 800,000 Rwandans were slaughtered in the span of just three months.

On April 6, 1994, ethnic Hutus throughout Rwanda began a killing spree that primarily targeted their Tutsi neighbors. By the time the genocide ended 100 days later, some 800,000 Tutsis and moderate Hutus had been murdered. The victims shown here were among an estimated 4,000 slaughtered in and around the church in the village of Nyarubuye.

## EXAMINING THE EXCUSES

Rarely do the major players involved completely acknowledge their part in either participating in genocide or letting it happen. A government may regret the loss of life, but it may also pass off large-scale killings as the natural result of civil conflict, often initiated by the group that was massacred. Foreign observers may defend their failure to intervene by arguing that violence is inevitable in certain regions (especially where ethnic or tribal groups have a long history of conflict), and they may insist that in such regions violence may flare up at any time and without warning, making a timely response difficult.

Such excuses do not apply to the events in Rwanda in 1994, as human rights advocates have pointed out. The Rwandan government could not pass off the genocide as the unfortunate by-product of a civil war; government officials laid the groundwork for and helped direct the killing. Likewise, the international community's failure to stop the genocide was shameful and inexcusable. Not only were there warning signs of impending large-scale violence in the months leading up to the genocide, but a UN-sponsored peacekeeping force was actually on the ground in Rwanda when the killing started.

Rwanda's two main ethnic groups, the majority Hutus and the minority Tutsis, had a centuries-long history of reasonably harmonious coexistence before 1959. That year, the Hutus fought successfully to end the system of Tutsi dominance that Belgian colonial rule had endorsed (Rwanda finally gained independence from Belgium in 1962). Thousands of Tutsis were killed, and approximately 150,000 fled the country, as a result of this fighting. After a decade of oppression and periodic massacres, perhaps 600,000 Tutsis—half of Rwanda's Tutsi population—had left the country. Yet it would not be totally accurate to say that relations between Hutus and the remaining Tutsis in Rwanda were unremittingly hostile. In some areas of the country, in fact, Hutus and Tutsis frequently intermarried, engaged in business ventures with one another, and lived side by side without incident.

In 1990 Tutsi exiles who had formed a rebel group, the Rwandan Patriotic Front (RPF), crossed into Rwanda from their bases in neighboring Uganda. In the ensuing civil war, the RPF managed to gain control of a significant part of northern Rwanda.

In July 1992, with encouragement from the United States, France, and the OAU, the warring parties first met in Tanzania in an effort to negotiate an end to the conflict. By August of the following year, the talks had produced an agreement, the Arusha Accords, which ended the civil war. The agreement called for

The bones of Rwanda genocide victims are displayed as a memorial at the former Murambi Technical School in Gikorongo. Some 10,000 who had sought refuge at the school were murdered there.

power sharing between the Hutus and the Tutsis, the repatriation of refugees, and rule by a transitional government until elections for a permanent government could be arranged. In October 1993 the United Nations Security Council authorized the establishment of a small peacekeeping force for the country, referred to as UNAMIR (the United Nations Assistance Mission for Rwanda).

Unfortunately, the transition to peace and stability anticipated by the Arusha Accords did not occur. On April 6, 1994, the plane carrying Rwandan president Juvenal Habyarimana and Burundian president Cyprien Ntaryamira was shot down as it approached the airport in the Rwandan capital of Kigali. Although it was never determined who carried out the assassinations of the presidents, both of whom were Hutus, the Tutsis were immediately blamed. The systematic killing of Tutsis and Hutu moderates began instantly, and then the genocide continued at a horrific rate throughout the month. Philip Gourevitch, author of *We Wish to Inform You That Tomorrow We Will Be Killed with Our Families*, reports that roughly 75 percent of the country's Tutsis had been murdered by early May. The killing had somewhat subsided by July, when the rebel RPF forces captured Kigali and secured control of the country.

## READING THE SIGNS

As horrific as the genocide turned out to be, there were definite signs before April 1994 that a racial purge could take place. One landmark report by Human Rights Watch/Africa spoke of the writing on the wall a year before the genocide. "Beyond the Rhetoric: Continuing Human Rights Abuses in Rwanda," published in March 1993, covered the findings of an international commission on human rights abuses in Rwanda. It was issued just a few months before the signing of the Arusha Accords seemed to signal that peace in Rwanda was at least possible. However, the report documented extensive government abuses against the Tutsis and widespread neglect for their rights, which should have dispelled any assumptions that the Tutsis' safety and protection were guaranteed.

The activities of the *interhamwe*, Hutu militia groups that carried out most of the killings in 1994, were well known in the years leading up to the genocide. They began forming in 1990 and, working with the support of the Rwandan government, conducted sporadic attacks on Tutsis. In late January 1993, more than 300 Tutsis were killed in a single attack led by the militias of the MRND (Mouvement Republicain National pour la Democratie et le Developpement) and the CDR (Committee for the Defense of the Republic). According to the Human Rights Watch/Africa report, between October 1990 and January 1993

## PROTECTING THE VICTIMS OF WAR

According to UNICEF, roughly 9 out of 10 people who die as the result of wars today are civilians. This reality is particularly devastating in Africa, a continent that has seen continuous war in recent decades. But the victims of Africa's many wars are not limited to those killed, or even those wounded. Conflict on the continent has created millions of refugees (people forced to flee their country) and internally displaced persons, or IDPs (people who remain in their country but have been forced from their homes).

By its very nature, war breaks down social norms, creating an atmosphere of brutality and chaos under which innocent people may be victimized, even when the combatants are members of a disciplined fighting force. The majority of African conflicts, however, are civil wars, and the rules of conventional warfare—rules designed, for example, to protect civilians from intentional harm—are not observed. Unquestionably, the chaos of conflict explains some atrocities perpetrated against African civilians in war zones. But many insurgent armies, and even government armies, deliberately target civilians in the pursuit of their strategic goals. Among the more horrific examples in recent years are the campaign of rape and amputation that maimed 8,000 people in Sierra Leone, the 1994 genocide in Rwanda, and the rape and looting in the Darfur region beginning in February 2003.

Perhaps the toughest responsibility for any UN agency working in Africa belongs to the High Commissioner for Refugees (UNHCR). The UNHCR reported that of the top 10 countries of refugee origin in 2004, 5 were African (Sudan, Burundi, the Democratic Republic of the Congo, Somalia, and Liberia). At the beginning of 2005, according to the UNHCR, there were more than 3 million refugees in Africa.

Refugee assistance is still lacking in many respects. As with other rights-related concerns, refugee assistance and protection in Africa suffers from a major gap between what is promised through conventional law and what is actually practiced. While the Universal Declaration of Human Rights guarantees the

"the Rwandan government had killed or caused to be killed about 2,000 of its citizens."

The militias had been using government-supplied arms since 1991. According to the HRW/Africa report, armament was part of a "self-defense" program, through which only supporters of Hutu Power—as the Hutu supremacist movement was called—

rights of people to leave their country, look for and receive asylum in another country, and change nationality if necessary, there are not yet legal instruments in place that handle this massive undertaking without relying heavily on international assistance. Because refugees are not native citizens, some governments still believe they can excuse themselves from their obligations.

It is a sad irony that Africa's internally displaced—people who have been uprooted but have remained within their country's borders—are greater in number than refugees but receive less protection. The Internal Displacement Monitoring Centre, an international group that advocates for the displaced, estimated that at the end of 2005 there were 12 million internally displaced persons in Africa—slightly more than half of the world's IDP population. Even with countries experiencing major resettlement operations—as in Angola, where 2 million IDPs were resettled following a 2002 peace agreement ending the country's long-running civil war—the continental total of displaced persons remains high because new crises are always unfolding and uprooting hundreds of thousands of people.

Sometimes displacement occurs for economic reasons. For example, the Internal Displacement Monitoring Centre reports that people in Sudan, Angola, Republic of the Congo, and Nigeria have been uprooted and moved because they lived in oil-rich areas where companies wanted to begin exploration or extraction. More often, however, displacement is caused by civil conflict or interstate war.

Neither the UNHCR nor other refugee agencies are officially mandated to assist IDPs, although they have offered their services whenever it aligns with their mission to refugees. The greatest obstacle in assisting this group is a lack of safety: while refugees have typically reached a place of relative safety where humanitarian groups are secure to set up a camp, IDPs usually are still vulnerable to attack. The threat to safety is the primary obstacle in the three countries with the highest number of IDPs in 2005, according to Internal Displacement Monitoring Centre estimates: Sudan (5.35 million), Uganda (1.74 million), and the Democratic Republic of the Congo (1.16 million). These people may fall victim to raiding, looting, abduction, and rape attacks by roaming militias and rebel armies.

were eligible to receive guns. "By late 1992, the militia had taken the lead in violence against Tutsi and members of the political opposition, thus 'privatizing' violence formerly carried out by the state itself," HRW/Africa noted. The further the government distanced itself from the violence, the easier it was to deny responsibility once the killings began. The Rwandan justice system, hardly a model of independence and impartiality, also neglected its primary responsibilities. On occasion, individuals who had committed abuses against Tutsis were arrested, but they were released quickly and their cases were never tried.

In the months before the genocide, the militias received government consent to establish control at the village level; one of the ways they accomplished this control was to erect road barriers. In a system that resembled the pass laws in South Africa, villagers were asked to present identity cards that showed whether they were Tutsi, Hutu, or Twa (a Pygmy group making up a small minority of Rwandans). Those who were not Hutu could be denied passage through a barrier and were subject to fines or beatings by militia members.

The HRW/Africa report concluded with recommendations for the international community, particularly France, which had supplied the Hutu leadership with arms. In order to help stop the

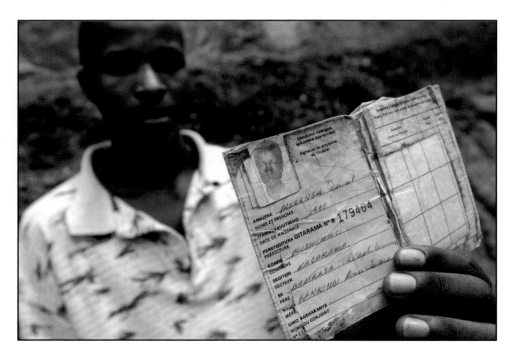

**Identity cards such as this one enabled members of Rwanda's minority Tutsi group to be easily identified by Hutu extremists.**

abuses, the report's authors recommended that Western countries "end military aid to both parties to the [civil] war" and make aid to the Rwandan government conditional on reforms. The Rwandan government was asked to dismantle the identity card system, to end the program of arming militias, and to bring to trial all those accused of killings and other human rights abuses. The government responded by creating its own human rights commission, whose sole purpose was to repudiate accusations of abuse and dress up the government's tarnished image.

Another significant recommendation that appeared in the HRW/Africa report was to end the growing propaganda campaign. Through various media outlets, Hutu leaders had spread hate messages to members of their ethnic group. One of the more popular anti-Tutsi pronouncements was the "Hutu Ten Commandments," compiled by a Hutu editor named Hassan Ngeze and published in December 1990 in his newspaper, *Kangura*. Among the directives were demands that Hutus show "unity and solidarity" against the "common Tutsi enemy"; that they consider a traitor any Hutu who "persecutes his brother Hutu"; and that they "stop having mercy on the Tutsis." The Hutu Ten Commandments were used to indoctrinate Hutus. "Community leaders across Rwanda regarded them as tantamount to law, and read them aloud at public meetings," writes Gourevitch.

The national radio station, RTLM, also played a pivotal rule in spreading propaganda. Broadcasters were blatantly anti-Tutsi in their reporting, urging Hutus to defend themselves against Tutsis, and then, beginning on April 6, to exterminate them. They explicitly directed their listeners to "go out there and kill" and "do their work" in shutting down the *inyenzi*—"cockroaches" in the national language, Kinyarwanda.

Like most propaganda, the messages of Hutu Power were built on myths and distortions about the Tutsis. The RTLM tried to convince the people that UNAMIR was not neutral but rather favored the RPF. President Habyarimana contributed to the propaganda by grossly exaggerating the RPF's crimes. During a speech delivered in March 1993, the president announced that the RPF had killed "several tens of thousands of citizens." Such rhetoric suggested that wiping out Tutsi civilians might be an appropriate and necessary response to the rebel problem.

# INTERNATIONAL NEGLECT

With an active peacekeeping mission in Rwanda, the United Nations appeared to be in a position to quell the violence that began on April 6, 1994. But that would require the UN to rein-force UNAMIR's small contingent of about 2,500 troops. Soon after the killing erupted, UNAMIR commander Major General Romeo Dallaire did in fact ask for additional peacekeeping sol-diers, but his superiors at UN headquarters in New York denied the request. Dallaire, a career officer in the Canadian army, believed that he could protect Rwanda's Tutsis with a relatively modest force. "I came to the United Nations from commanding a mechanized brigade group of 5,000 soldiers," he said a few months after the atrocities. "If I had had that brigade group in Rwanda, there would be hundreds of thousands of lives spared today."

Instead of sending more peacekeepers, the United Nations actually drew down the UNAMIR force, to a mere 270 by the second week of the genocide. The UN member state with the strongest military, the United States, had persuaded other states against intervention. This move by President Bill Clinton's administration, which some cite as one of the worst cases of rights neglect by the United States in recent decades, was strong-ly influenced by the failure of a U.S. peacekeeping mission in Somalia.

In the Battle of Mogadishu, fought just six months before vio-lence broke out in Rwanda, 18 U.S. soldiers were killed in a fire-

Rwandan soldiers assigned to the African Union peacekeeping mission in Darfur prepare to board transport planes at the airport in Kigali, November 2005. Hampered by insufficient numbers of troops, logistical difficulties, and weak rules of engagement, the AU peacekeeping mission in Sudan was widely regarded as ineffective. Some rights advocates charged that, a decade later, the world had still not learned the lessons of the Rwanda catastrophe.

fight with Somali militia fighters and throngs of angry civilians. News broadcasts showed one dead U.S. soldier being dragged through the city's streets by an angry mob, a scene that made some horrified Americans anxious about future military operations in Africa. Mark Bowden, author of *Black Hawk Down*, explains how the disaster set a precedent for peacekeeping: "When Washington policymakers consider sending soldiers into foreign crisis zones, there is invariably a caveat: Remember Somalia."

In the aftermath of the Rwanda genocide, there was considerable hand-wringing over the world's failure to stop the slaughter.

Former U.S. president Bill Clinton with children in Kigali, July 2005. During an earlier visit to the Rwandan capital, Clinton apologized for the failure of the international community to stop the 1994 genocide. "We did not act quickly enough after the killing began. . . . We did not immediately call these crimes by their rightful name: genocide," Clinton said.

In March 1998 President Clinton traveled to Kigali and apologized to the Rwandan people. "The international community . . . must bear its share of responsibility for this tragedy," he said. "We did not act quickly enough after the killing began. . . . We did not immediately call these crimes by their rightful name: genocide." While he acknowledged that what had happened in Rwanda could not be undone, Clinton called on the world to respond more vigorously should similar circumstances arise in the future. "Genocide can occur anywhere," he said. "It is not an African phenomenon. We must have global vigilance. And never again must we be shy in the face of the evidence."

A few months after Clinton's speech, the UN secretary-general, Kofi Annan, also issued an apology in Kigali. "The world must deeply repent this failure," Annan said. "Rwanda's tragedy was the world's tragedy. All of us who cared about Rwanda, all of us who witnessed its suffering, fervently wish that we could have prevented the genocide. Looking back now, we see the signs which then were not recognized. Now we know that what we did was not nearly enough—not enough to save Rwanda from itself, not enough to honor the ideals for which the United Nations exists. We will not deny that, in their greatest hour of need, the world failed the people of Rwanda. . . ."

A mere five years after President Clinton and Secretary-General Annan apologized for the world's inaction in the face of the Rwanda genocide, and less than a decade since that genocide had taken place, large-scale killing began in the Darfur region of Sudan. Once again, however, the international community failed to take timely and forceful action to stop the slaughter.

# PROSECUTION AND RECONCILIATION

In many cases a court of justice stands as the last opportunity to address human rights abuse. After victims have spoken out, advocacy groups have done all they can to expose violations, and commissions have completed their investigations, it is the court's turn to issue the final word. The most serious abuses in Africa—crimes against humanity, war crimes, and genocide—have either been tried by temporary courts, such as the International Criminal Tribunal for Rwanda (ICTR), or they have fallen under the jurisdiction of the newly formed International Criminal Court (ICC). To ensure that many other abuses are prosecuted as well, an African regional court has also been forming since 1998. In some countries in which the need for reconciliation is particularly urgent, national governments have bypassed all available systems of justice to establish truth commissions—an approach first taken in post-apartheid South Africa.

# INTERNATIONAL CRIMINAL COURT

The international court system dates back to the World War II era. In the Moscow Declaration of 1943, the leaders of the United States, Great Britain, and the Soviet Union announced their determination to prosecute war criminals. In 1945 the victorious Allies set up the first international court, the Nuremberg Tribunal, which was an ad hoc court established to try Nazi war criminals.

The International Criminal Tribunal for Rwanda, set up by the United Nations in 1994, was the first court to try individuals for genocide and related crimes committed in Africa. The ICTR, which is based in Arusha, Tanzania, originally intended to indict all those who planned or helped carry out the genocide, but soon realized that with nearly half a million estimated suspects, there were far too many cases to handle. Trials would be held only for the genocide's ringleaders, while the Rwandan government would assume jurisdiction over the tens of thousands of lower-level killers who had not yet been brought to justice. No conviction by the ICTR may carry the death penalty, although that is a possible sentence in the Rwandan courts.

The thousands of other suspects who still have not faced trial will be prosecuted in Rwanda's *gacaca* courts, a legal system based on traditional African law. Set up in 2001, the *gacaca* system holds trials at the village level, with community members serving on the juries. This solution will eventually cut down the enormous backlog of detainees, but it has also drawn criticism from legal experts who say the judges are not adequately trained and the court system is biased.

As early as the creation of the Nuremberg Tribunal, world leaders had pushed for the creation of a permanent international criminal court. Until 1998 the UN Security Council had

Judges of the International Criminal Court listen to arguments at a preliminary hearing in connection with the case of a militia leader in the Democratic Republic of the Congo, March 2006. A permanent court based in The Hague, the ICC has jurisdiction to try cases of serious human rights violations when national judicial systems are unable or unwilling to do so.

established tribunals that were only temporary, intended for individual countries in which the most serious crimes were committed. When the UN member states finally adopted the Rome Statute of the International Criminal Court, the newly formed body began preparing to conduct investigations. As of spring 2006, the ICC had opened investigations into crimes in the Democratic Republic of the Congo, Uganda, and Darfur. It also received a referral, in January 2005, to investigate crimes in the Central African Republic.

Individual countries still have primary jurisdiction to rule on any and all charges; the ICC will step in only when states "are unable or unwilling to investigate or prosecute." In the case of Sierra Leone, which was willing to prosecute crimes committed during its horrific 11-year civil war, the government and the

United Nations worked together to establish a special court. This court, which since 2002 has held trials in Freetown, Sierra Leone, is founded on the combination of the Sierra Leonean and international law systems.

The ICC is still young and has yet to prove itself as a facilitator—or, if necessary, the final arbiter—of international justice. One of its greatest obstacles has been extradition, because many of the most serious offenders manage to find refuge in other countries. However, the advantage of a permanent body like the ICC is that it can begin trying criminals in a shorter time than is needed for an ad hoc court to establish itself.

**Charles Taylor appears before the Special Tribunal for Sierra Leone in Freetown, April 3, 2006. Taylor, the former president of Liberia, had been indicted on 17 counts of war crimes and crimes against humanity. The charges stem from his role in fomenting a brutal civil war in neighboring Sierra Leone.**

## THE ICC'S BIGGEST OPPONENT

In recent years, one of the most significant issues related to human rights is the U.S. resistance to the ICC. Although the United States signed the Rome Statute in 1998 that established the international court, it has refused to ratify it. The biggest point of contention is the UN's refusal to grant immunity to U.S. soldiers in peacekeeping missions, a concession that the United States insists is necessary to prevent politically motivated prosecutions.

Various UN member states have stuck to their guns on the issue, arguing that altering the ICC's jurisdiction in any way would corrupt the court's integrity. The standoff has had serious consequences. As part of the U.S. Servicemembers Civil Relief Act (2003), the U.S. government has even denied military aid to countries that support the ICC.

In the human rights arena, observers wonder if this debate will slow down the justice process. When, in 2005, the administration of George W. Bush proposed an ad hoc court for Sudan in lieu of an ICC tribunal, human rights groups accused the United States of stalling justice for the people of Darfur. They argued that the time and resources needed for a new court were a waste in light of what a permanent court could do sooner. Some believe that if the United States continues to undermine the ICC, the country's reputation as a human rights advocate will suffer. "The ICC is potentially the most important human rights institution of the last 50 years," says Human Rights Watch. "The continued opposition of the United States, a long-time champion of international justice, will cast a long shadow over America's credibility as a champion of human rights and justice worldwide."

## THE AFRICAN COURT

At its creation the African Commission on Human and Peoples' Rights pledged itself to protect Africans' rights. Yet until recently there were no mechanisms to effectively carry out this objective. Some experts believe that the African Charter (1981) was inherently flawed because it did not include a proper court in the original plan for the African Commission. The absence of a court distinguished the African Commission from its two regional counterparts, the Council of Europe and the Organization of American States, which included the European Court of Human

Rights and the Inter-American Court of Human Rights, respectively, in their original framework.

Before a protocol was adopted in 1998 to set up the African Court, the African Commission had fielded complaints of abuse or neglect, but it had done so at a staggeringly slow pace. Julia Harrington, co-director of the Institute for Human Rights and Development in Africa, headquartered in The Gambia, reports that between 1986 and 2000, the African Commission reviewed on average fewer than 20 complaints per year.

The African Court on Human and Peoples' Rights may solve that problem and serve as a solid foundation for a regional justice system. As of May 2006, however, the African Court had not yet heard any cases, and advocacy groups such as Human Rights

A survivor of the Rwanda genocide is led away from pink-clad suspects in Butare, 2002. She was among those asked to identify people who had participated in the killings, in preparation for their trials before traditional *gacaca* courts.

# RWANDA'S GACACA COURTS

In 2001 the proposed *gacaca* courts offered a new method of handling the backlog of suspects in the Rwanda genocide. Unlike the European-based conventional courts, these courts are based on a traditional system (*gacaca* loosely translates as "justice on the grass"). Village residents settle disputes through a straightforward process: they hear the case, during which the suspect can present his or her defense, and then the jurors base a final ruling on a majority vote. For the millions who have waited too long for justice, the *gacaca* courts help Rwandans imagine a day when this embattled nation can finally heal.

However, even though they operate at a much faster pace than the ICTR, *gacaca* courts still have suffered delays. The pretrial phase did not end until February 2005 for a majority of courts. It has been reported that hearings may take between three and five years—or even longer if the original estimates of total suspects were too low. Much of the delay stems from having to prepare the courts, since the massive number of cases demanded that ordinary citizens undergo training to take on the duties of judges.

Several complaints have been lodged against this system. Observers claim that the judges' training is not adequate and that the courts are biased, focusing too heavily on the crimes of Hutu Power while ignoring the crimes of the Rwandan Patriotic Front, the Tutsi rebel force whose members were also reported to have slaughtered unarmed civilians. In addition, critics wonder how long jury members can serve, since most are not being financially compensated for their service.

Others have faith in the *gacaca* system despite its flaws. It is, after all, the continuation of an African tradition that has worked for centuries. Furthermore, by staging the court trials in the communities in which most of the crimes took place, the chances are much greater that eyewitnesses will be available to ensure fair proceedings.

Watch and Amnesty International were concerned that the court's human rights focus might be diluted as the result of decisions taken by the African Union.

# THE RECONCILIATION MODEL

Some countries have come up with alternative legal solutions that do not require regional or international courts to hold trials.

This approach may apply to a country that has finally committed itself to addressing the rights abuses of the past, yet also has foreseen the limitations of such an undertaking. The abuses may be too buried in history, or may simply be too numerous, to punish every offender. As Richard Goldstone, former chief prosecutor for the UN International Criminal Tribunal for Rwanda, stated: "If one had to bring to court all the perpetrators of human rights abuses during the last 40 years, there just would not be enough courts to deal with it." The reconciliation approach also may be appropriate if relations between former enemies are still volatile. Such were the circumstances in South Africa when the government set up its Truth and Reconciliation Commission (TRC) in 1996.

It was clear that the worst crimes of apartheid deserved harsh punishments, but as Archbishop Desmond Tutu points out, such an approach might have sparked terrible reprisals. "We could very well have had justice, retributive justice, and had a South Africa lying in ashes," he wrote in his recollection of Africa's period of reconstruction, *No Future Without Forgiveness*.

Truth initiatives still acknowledge the suffering of victims, but unlike courts of justice, they do not impose the full penalty on perpetrators. Post-apartheid South Africa paved the way in this direction with its TRC, which held trials to address the crimes and violations committed during the apartheid years. The TRC helped inspire the creation of other truth commissions in Burundi, Rwanda, Liberia, and Sierra Leone.

Headed by Tutu, a Nobel Peace Prize winner and champion of reconciliation in South Africa, the TRC included three separate boards: the Human Rights Violations Committee, the Committee on Amnesty, and the Reparation and Rehabilitation Committee. The Human Rights Violations Committee offered amnesty to individuals who presented a full disclosure of abuses they carried out between 1960 and 1994.

**Desmond Tutu presents the five-volume report of South Africa's Truth and Reconciliation Commission to President Nelson Mandela, October 1998. To avoid tearing apart its fragile democracy, South Africa opted to forgo full retributive justice for crimes committed under the apartheid regime.**

The TRC trials ultimately led to a more truthful account of abuse than could have been achieved in a conventional court. Because witnesses were not bound to questioning by prosecutors, they were free to tell their stories of abuse completely; because offenders received amnesty only if they offered full disclosure, they were obliged to give a full account of their crimes as well.

More than a decade after the creation of the TRC, South Africa seems to have established the foundations of a stable democracy where the human rights of all citizens are promoted and protected. It has avoided the tragic cycle experienced by so many African countries in the postcolonial era, whereby one brutal regime that abuses and oppresses is replaced by another that commits its own abuses, often against the former regime's supporters. This cycle regularly plunges African nations into war and police-state situations, creating the conditions that allow human rights abuse to flourish.

Ending this cycle continent-wide would require far-reaching efforts on the national, regional, and international levels. Only through the combination of effective relief efforts, UN resolutions and economic sanctions, meaningful peacemaking operations, constitutional reforms, rights advocacy, and a comprehensive and fair justice system can Africa's leaders be brought closer to fulfilling their obligations to their people.

# GLOSSARY

**AD HOC**—designed for a particular end or an issue at hand.

**ASYLUM**—protection granted to a refugee of another country.

**AUTONOMY**—the state of being self-governing.

**CHATTEL SLAVERY**—the oldest form of slavery, in which slaves are owned and traded according to traditional practice.

**CONSCRIPTION**—compulsory recruitment for military service.

**DEMOBILIZE**—to remove from military service.

**EMANCIPATE**—to free from bondage.

**EXTRADITION**—the legal surrender of a fugitive to the jurisdiction of another government for trial.

**FULL DISCLOSURE**—the admission of all relevant information.

**GACACA**—a traditional system of justice in Africa.

**GENOCIDE**—the deliberate and systematic destruction of a racial, political, or cultural group.

**PROPAGANDA**—the spreading of ideas or allegations to support one cause or damage an opposing cause.

**REMUNERATION**—payment for goods or services.

**SIGNATORY**—a government bound with others by a signed agreement or convention.

**SOVEREIGNTY**—freedom from external control.

# FURTHER READING

An-Na'im, Abdullahi Ahmed, and Francis M. Deng, eds. *Human Rights in Africa: Cross-Cultural Perspectives.* Washington, D.C.: The Brookings Institution, 1990.

De Waal, Alex, and Yoanes Ajawin, eds. *When Peace Comes: Civil Society and Development in Sudan.* Lawrenceville, N.J.: The Red Sea Press, 2002.

Evans, Malcolm D., and Rachel Murray, eds. *The African Charter on Human and Peoples' Rights: The System in Practice, 1986–2000.* Cambridge, UK: Cambridge University Press, 2002.

Gourevitch, Philip. *We Wish to Inform You That Tomorrow We Will Be Killed with Our Families.* New York: Picador, 1998.

Graybill, Lyn. *Truth and Reconciliation in South Africa: Miracle or Model?* Boulder, Colo.: Lynne Rienner Publishers, 2002.

Mandela, Nelson. *Long Walk to Freedom.* Boston: Little, Brown and Co., 1994.

McCarthy-Arnolds, Eileen; David R. Penna; and Debra Joy Cruz Sobrepeña, eds. *Africa, Human Rights, and the Global System.* Westport, Conn.: Greenwood Press, 1994.

Press, Robert M. *The New Africa: Dispatches from a Changing Continent.* Gainesville: University Press of Florida, 1999.

Salam, A. H. Abdel, and Alex de Waal, eds. *The Phoenix State: Civil Society and the Future of Sudan.* Lawrenceville, N.J.: The Red Sea Press, 2001.

**FURTHER READING**

# INTERNET RESOURCES

**HTTP://HRW.ORG/DOC/?T=AFRICA**

Reports on various human rights issues in Africa. Each country also has its own page.

**HTTP://WWW.IABOLISH.COM/**

Website of group devoted to eradicating slavery worldwide.

**HTTP://WWW.UN.ORG/RIGHTS/**

This rights overview includes an online version of the Universal Declaration of Human Rights.

**HTTP://WWW.CHILD-SOLDIERS.ORG/**

The home page of this group serves as an introduction to the countries where children are recruited as soldiers.

**HTTP://WWW.FREEDOMHOUSE.ORG/TEMPLATE.CFM?PAGE=1**

This Internet resource offers a picture of rights conditions throughout the world by rating the "progress and decline of political rights and civil liberties."

# FOR MORE INFORMATION

## AMNESTY INTERNATIONAL

5 Penn Plaza
14th Floor
New York, NY 10001
Phone: (212) 807-8400
E-mail: admin-us@aiusa.org
Website: http://web.amnesty.org/library/engworld/2af

## HUMAN RIGHTS WATCH

350 Fifth Ave.
34th Floor
New York, NY 10118-3299
Phone: (212) 290-4700
E-mail: hrwnyc@hrw.org
Website: http://www.hrw.org/

## AMERICAN ANTI-SLAVERY GROUP

198 Tremont St., #421
Boston, MA 02116
Phone: 1-800-884-0719
E-mail: info@iabolish.com
Website: http://www.iabolish.com/

## UNITED NATIONS HIGH COMMISSIONER FOR HUMAN RIGHTS

Administrative Section
Office of the United Nations High Commissioner for Human
Rights

Palais des Nations
CH-1211 Geneva 10, Switzerland
Fax: + 41 22 917 90 24
E-mail: personnel@ohchr.org
Website: http://www.ohchr.org/english

## AFRICAN COMMISSION ON HUMAN AND PEOPLES' RIGHTS

Kairaba Ave.
PO Box 673
Banjul, The Gambia
Phone: (220) 392 962
E-mail: achpr@achpr.org
Website: http://www.achpr.org/

## BUREAU OF AFRICAN AFFAIRS

2201 C St., NW, Room 5242A
Washington, DC 20520
Phone: (202) 647-3502
Fax: (202) 736-4583
Website: http://www.state.gov/p/af/ci/

## AFRICA ACTION

1634 Eye St., NW, #810
Washington, DC 20006
Phone: (202) 546-7961
Fax: (202) 546-1545
Email: africaaction@igc.org
Website: http://www.africaaction.org/index.php

# INDEX

Numbers in **bold italic** refer to captions.

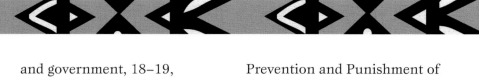

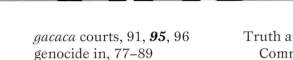

# PICTURE CREDITS

**Front cover:** Top Photos (left to right): Stephanie Welsh/Getty Images; Per-Anders Pettersson/Getty Images; Anna Zieminski/AFP/Getty Images; Main Photo: Spencer Platt/Getty Images

**Back cover:** Collage of images created by OTTN Publishing with images provided by US AID

# CONTRIBUTORS

**PROFESSOR ROBERT I. ROTBERG** is Director of the Program on Intrastate Conflict and Conflict Resolution at the Kennedy School, Harvard University, and President of the World Peace Foundation. He is the author of a number of books and articles on Africa, including *A Political History of Tropical Africa* and *Ending Autocracy, Enabling Democracy: The Tribulations of Southern Africa.*

**BRIAN BAUGHAN** is a freelance writer and editor living in northeast Philadelphia. He has also served as contributing editor to study guides on Italo Calvino and Thomas Mann in Professor Howard Bloom's Major Short Story Writers series. This is his first book.